BUDDY BAKER

*Big Band Arranger, Disney Legend
& Musical Genius*

Ben Ohmart
Foreword by Lou Bellson

BearManor Media

Albany, Georgia

Buddy Baker: Big Band Arranger, Disney Legend & Musical Genius
Copyright © 2016 Ben Ohmart. All Rights Reserved.

No part of this book may be reproduced in any form or by any means, electronic, mechanical, digital, photocopying or recording, except for the inclusion in a review, without permission in writing from the publisher.

All photos are from the Buddy Baker estate, unless noted.

This text and book are not endorsed by the Walt Disney Company. Any Disney characters contained in any photo are the property of the Disney company.

Published in the USA by
BearManor Media
P.O. Box 71426
Albany, GA 31708
www.BearManorMedia.com

Softcover Edition
ISBN-10: 1593931956
ISBN-13: 978-1-59393-195-7

Printed in the United States of America

*For Buddy, Charlotte, Noreene,
and every Disney fan who ever screamed
in the Haunted Mansion elevator*

Table of Contents

Foreword ix

Introduction xi

Chapter 1: The Missouri Gentleman 1

Chapter 2: Young Man Goes West 19

Chapter 3: Wicked Woman 29

Chapter 4: Scoring Disney 41

Chapter 5: Familyland, Disneyland 53

Chapter 6: The Haunted Mansion 75

Chapter 7: After Walt 79

Chapter 8: Third Time Charm 93

Chapter 9: EPCOT 101

Chapter 10: Not Retired 109

Credits 141

Foreword

In 1947, I was playing drums for Tommy Dorsey at the Casino Gardens in California. Marty Berman, baritone sax player in the band, drove me to work every day. One day, Marty gave me an album of Herb Jeffries singing with an orchestral background by Buddy Baker. I was quite favorably impressed by Buddy's writing.

Later, Marty, who knew Buddy, arranged a meeting between Buddy and me. We were like brothers from the beginning. I started lessons with Buddy immediately as his knowledge of the orchestra was phenomenal. He gave me scores by Ravel, Delius and Stravinsky to study. Whatever I wrote, Buddy analyzed my works and showed me ways to improve.

Buddy Baker has always been one of the select composers in Hollywood. He arranged for Kay Kyser, Harry James, Tommy Dorsey and every top band. He arranged for star vocalists including Ella Fitzgerald, Dinah Shore and my late wife, Pearl Bailey.

While I played for Harry James, I happened to mention that one of my lessons from Buddy was "42 ways to play a G7 chord." Harry was amazed; he was immediately transformed into a Buddy Baker fan.

In 1954, when Norman Granz asked me to record something unique, I called upon Buddy Baker for ideas. Buddy suggested I write 12 original compositions which he then would arrange. The first 6 pieces included 26 woodwinds and featured alto saxophone leads Willie Smith and Willie Schwartz. The other 6 pieces involved a large string ensemble. The resulting album, *Journey into Love*, remains as fresh and dynamic today as ever.

Buddy wrote for Walt Disney Studios for almost 30 years; and he composed prolifically for Disneyland in California and Disney World in Florida.

Even today he teaches film scoring at USC and conducts workshops at New York University during the summer. Buddy Baker is a true genius of his craft. He continues to give his students and fans the best music there is. Besides all of this, he is a warm and dedicated person who is loved by everyone.

Louie Bellson
June 2002

Introduction

The most unfortunate thing about this book is that Buddy died six months after I began interviewing him for it. He was the most cordial gentleman I've ever been privileged to interview, and he was ready to keep going indefinitely with my questioning for x amount of months until enough material had been collected. His wife Charlotte was also up and positive about the whole project. They were a couple who joyously gave of their limited time.

Then Buddy died. Charlotte lost her best friend and it devastated her, as it did us all. His passing was completely unexpected and, though he was 84 years old, utterly untimely. Buddy Baker was energetic, loved to work, loved to help, and he was full of stories. It is with sadness that he never got to see this book complete—or finish his story—but rather than shelf this project (which I did for more than a decade, I'm sorry to say; that's how hard it was to complete this work without Buddy around), I wanted to see the pieces put together as a tribute to a man whose work I've always greatly admired.

As a kid, I loved Disney movies. Not just the ordinary classics like *The Love Bug* and *Cinderella*, but specifically that company's post-Walt greatness—the era I grew up with—which include far more goodies than film historians ever credit. If I had to choose, I'd pick *Alice in Wonderland*, *Pete's Dragon* and *Gus* as my top three favorite Disney films. Because as a child, these captured an innocence in their magic that is sadly lacking in Disney's current fare of farting, burping and sarcasm jokes that hardly sets it apart from any other film factory. But then, the world has changed. Now piercings and tattoos are considered beautiful, and the most important asset is "youth" for a kid's film, so obviously though I was only born in 1970, I am already "past it." But back when there was a difference between a kid's film and a family film, when a kid's film didn't even have to have kids in it (*Gus*, *The Love Bug*), there was also a special Disney "sound" that Buddy Baker helped create.

Originally, I wanted to do a music book on the three B's of Disney music of my favorite time period (post-Disney, pre-Eisner): Baker, Brunner and Bruns. I couldn't locate the family of George Bruns (composer of *The Love Bug* and "Yo Ho Yo Ho, A Pirate's Life for Me"). Robert Brunner (composer of *That Darn*

Introduction

Cat, and the wonderful Dexter Riley trilogy: *The Computer Wore Tennis Shoes, Now You See Him, Now You Don't, The Strongest Man in the World*) seemed too busy or indifferent to the idea. That left Buddy Baker. He was easy to reach, and helpful. A few years before this, in 1999, he had written me a long letter thanking me

UNIVERSITY
OF SOUTHERN
CALIFORNIA

September 4, 1999

School of Music

Scoring for Motion
Pictures and Television

Dr. Buddy Baker
Director

Advisory Board
Buddy Baker
Richard Bellis
Charles Bernstein
Elmer Bernstein
Larry Blank
Bill Conti
Hoyt Curtin
Linda Danly
Jerry Goldsmith
Joe Harnell
Ron Jones
Morten Lauridsen
Robert Linn
Cynthia Millar
John Parker
Mike Post
Eric Prendergast
David Raksin
David Shire
Jack Smalley
David Spear
Fred Steiner
John Williams
Christopher Young

Mr. Ben Ohmart
P.O.Box 750
Boalsburg, PA 16827

Dear Ben:

What a nice flattering letter! Letters like yours makes it all feel like the time and effort was worth it when you hear from someone who appreciates what we used to do at Disney. Our aim was always toward quality and taste.

I'm still writing for the Theme Park division of Disney (WDI). Just finished "Innoventions" for Disneyland, "Winnie the Pooh" for Walt Disney World and "The Seven Voyages of Sindbad" for Disney's Tokyo Seas.

I'm sending you a lead sheet of "Grim Grinning Ghosts"--the main theme of the Haunted Mansion attraction at Disneyland, Walt Disney World, Tokyo Disneyland and Euro-Disneyland in Paris, France. Also – I'm including a lead sheet of the Baby Fox theme from "The Fox and the Hound" (animated feature) for your father, John.

Best regards,

Buddy Baker

University of
Southern California
Los Angeles,
California 90089-0851
Tel: 213 740 7416
Fax: 213 740 3217

for my fan letter and told me what he was up to (working on Pooh for Tokyo Disneyland). He also completely filled out my enclosed blank sheet of music paper with a handwritten lead sheet of the *Haunted Mansion* theme, which is personally the most valuable thing I own. I treasure that sheet.

While interviewing Buddy for this book, it was my supreme pleasure also to put him in touch with an idol to us both, Frances Langford, with whom he worked in the glory days of radio. Charlotte Baker said it made his day. I was happy to give something back to the Master. Buddy stated, "Frances remembered the times we spent together on the Hope show. I didn't mention to her that I had been with Disney for 29 years and USC for 14 years as Director of the film music program. We talked mostly about those of us who are left and of many who are no longer around."

We all miss you, Buddy.

This is not a Disney book. There are plenty of works covering the history of Disney, Disneyland, Disneyworld, and within them all, Disney music. This is about a man and his music, who also worked for Disney. Every quote in here, unless otherwise stated, is Buddy talking. While this book isn't as complete as it would have been—had we not been robbed of Buddy's style, grace and humor—I feel it's close. And I hope you enjoy reading about one of the greatest film composers in history.

Huge thanks go to Noreene Doss who, even when Buddy was alive, provided some of the most detailed and precise information (including the early Baker family history) in this book. Phil Roper, Dr. James Jameson, Alan Oldfield and Dr. Payton Kelly provided

INTRODUCTION

invaluable memories of Buddy's early years in Springfield, Missouri. And thanks to Dieter Salemann for his helpful information on Exclusive Records.

Ben Ohmart
August 2015

It is one thing to be the composer of a popular song that finds its way to #1 for a while and then winds its way to nostalgia, taken out ever so often to be remembered. It's another thing to pen a "White Christmas" that is beloved by families and lovers every year without fail. But there are few, very few music gods that are able to construct tunes that are performed every waking hour, every day of the year, from childhood to wistful adulthood. Buddy Baker lorded over Olympus for years.

Alan Oldfield, longtime friend

CHAPTER 1
The Missouri Gentleman

Thomas Woodford "Woody" Baker was born on March 25, 1895 in Texas County, Missouri. His father, Charles Pierce Baker, came to Missouri from Culpepper County, Virginia, in 1856. His mother, Emily C. Bray Baker, came to Missouri from Randolph County, North Carolina in 1861. They were married in Texas County, Missouri on February 3, 1876.

Woody was the eighth of eleven children. His father was a farmer and carpenter. He attended Grandview School and graduated from the eighth grade. He worked on the farm with his father, and, as a young man, worked in the hay fields in Kansas during the summer. He had a heart attack and died on August 21, 1953, while driving down "old" Highway 66.

Martha Marilda "Rilda" Johnson Baker was born on September 24, 1892 in Green County, Missouri. Her father was Joseph Curtis Jackson Johnson who was a lifelong resident of Greene County near Ash Grove, Missouri. Her mother was Alberta Jane Daniel Johnson who came to Greene County, Missouri from Kansas as a small child. They were married on July 30, 1885, and lived to celebrate their 50th wedding anniversary.

Rilda was the oldest of six sisters; the first baby girl died in infancy and one brother died at age 14. Her father was a veterinarian and part-time constable. She attended Kelly School and graduated from the eighth grade. As a young girl, she worked as a telephone operator at Walnut Grove, Missouri, which is approximately 8-10 miles from her home in Ash Grove. She had a heart attack and died on April 14, 1964 in St. John's Hospital in Springfield.

Woody and Rilda lived in the same area near Ash Grove. They met at a party and were married on September 22, 1915. Norman D. "Buddy" Baker was born on

January 4, 1918, and Noreene Baker on January 7, 1922. Noreene was to be named Martha Jane after her mother and grandmother. His mother read to Buddy often and on one occasion read about a girl named "Noreene" who was very special, so he began calling his little sister "Noreene."

Buddy stated, "My mom was a little overweight when I was in school in Springfield. Later she trimmed down to be a very

Woody and Rilda Baker.

slim person. I inherited most of my traits from my mom. She was very organized, frugal, a perfectionist and of an 'ahead' thinking mind-set. My dad was a heavy-set jokester, carefree and more freewheeling with as few worries as possible."

Soon after Noreene was born, Woody and Rilda moved to Springfield, Missouri. Woody's first job was in the Parts Department for the International Harvester Company. As an "outside" person, he could not stand the confinement and took a job as a salesman for the Davis Candy Company where he traveled a large territory selling candy wholesale for several years. He was offered a job as a route salesman for Willow Springs Creamery which later became Borden's and subsequently Pilley's Creamery. His first route was retailing to homes—when milk came in glass bottles.

Little Buddy worked with him at one point. "Bud cut off his finger on his left hand one time," Noreene explains. "He was taking some milk bottles up to a home and a utility company had taken out something similar to a telephone pole and someone had covered it with grass. Bud stepped in that hole, and of course there were rocks around it. And the rocks broke the glass, and it cut right across the knuckle on the third finger of his left hand. They were a block from Burge Hospital, so Dad took him over to have it sewed on, and it didn't seem to give him any problems after that."

Later, Woody had a wholesale route to businesses and grocery stores. He was a "dyed-in-the-wool" Baptist, and had one brother, Dewey, who was a Baptist minister. Woody enjoyed singing in the church choir although he did not read music. He enjoyed taking part in school plays since he and Rilda were both active in the PTA (Parent-Teacher Association) when Buddy and Noreene were in elementary school. He had few culinary talents; his only one was popping popcorn which the children would enjoy nightly.

"Mother was more reserved than Dad," recalls Noreene, "probably because of having asthma all of her life. She was an excellent seamstress and made all of our clothes until we were 'big' kids. She was an excellent cook (in those days, using lard, butter, and cream) and always had cookies and goodies when we came home from school. She enjoyed many kinds of handiwork including tatting, crocheting, knitting, embroidery, and she also

Young Buddy and Noreene.

made hairpin lace. She was always available to work at the polls on election day, too. She was a Sunday School teacher and also a Baptist. She played the piano for her own enjoyment and had previously played for church. She was great at making birthday cakes.

"Our home was a simple, pleasant, loving home. Our lives were centered around our home, school and church. Dad provided for our family—we had plenty of food and clothes and a warm home. Mother was always at home to greet us with a big hug when we arrived home from school."

Buddy recalled, "My folks were great for each other because of their very different personalities. My dad was a very outgoing type of person. He enjoyed the outdoors with hunting and fishing trips, ball games, gardening, singing in the church choir and visiting family. He was a very carefree soul. My mother was just the opposite. A proud lady who loved being at home, loved tatting, quilting, flowers, church and all the more sedate things. She played piano for the church services. She took care of all the family business, taxes, mortgages, etc. Noreene and I had a great family relationship within our home."

Buddy and Noreene.

"Since Buddy was four years older than me," says Noreene, "he contracted all of the childhood diseases—measles, mumps, chicken pox—and brought them home from school so that I had them all before I even started school!"

Buddy started piano lessons at age 4 when their next door neighbor, a piano teacher, began teaching the prodigy simple exercises. Buddy could read notes before he could read words. Luckily for him, there was already a piano in the house since his mother enjoyed playing (though he learned more from their neighbor than his mother). Buddy moved to the trumpet at age 11. Buddy and Noreene attended Berry Elementary School, Pipkin Junior High School, and Senior High School (now Central High School). The family was active in the Robberson Avenue Baptist Church where Buddy was baptized on April 14, 1929 and where Woody was a deacon.

Buddy's Boy Scout Troop #9 was sponsored by the church. As a young man he played the trumpet in the church orchestra as well as in the Boy Scout Band and the school band at Pipkin Junior High. He had studied trumpet under Southwest Missouri State musician Winston Lynes who ended up studying under Buddy years later in California when the composer/arranger was working for Disney.

Longtime Springfield friend Jim Jameson recalled Buddy's great ear for music. "Sitting in the balcony of Denton's Drug Store at South and McDaniel, he was amazing. It just took him a few minutes and Buddy would complete a whole arrangement without ever going near a piano."

"I could read music before I could read English," Buddy

explained. "No, I wasn't a prodigy. I had music around all the time. Everything sort of revolved around the church."

Young Buddy Baker.

"After school, work, practicing music lessons and dinner," says Noreene, "we would listen to our favorite radio programs, play games, work jigsaw puzzles, or read—then it was popcorn time!

"Bud always liked cars. He progressed through toy cars, tinker toys, marbles, red wagons, baseball with the neighborhood kids on the dead-end street, bicycles, and taking care of 'Coke,' his Shetland pony which he won by collecting Coca-Cola bottle caps. His first car was a Model A Ford with a rumble seat. He later had a LaSalle, a classy red Dodge, an MG which he drove from California to Missouri, and many other cars to follow."

Buddy in his baseball uniform.

There was always an attitude of caring between Buddy and Noreene. When she was very young, he always had her by the hand everywhere they went. That same love permeated through their adult lives as long as their parents lived and continued until Buddy's last day.

"We shall always be grateful for our wonderful childhood," states Noreene, "which was built on family and love."

"Going to school, I had a lot of friends," said Buddy. "It was a normal childhood. We didn't move around a lot. I went to grade school for 6 years, then on to junior high school for the next 3 years, then on into high school. In grade school there wasn't much music to do. I studied piano when I was 4 and I got into classical

Buddy and Noreene and friends.

music. But I got to thinking: for boys, playing piano was sort of a sissy thing to do. I had a cousin who was a good trumpet player, and he talked to me about playing trumpet. So I finally got a trumpet, took lessons on it, and became a trumpet player. I didn't play piano professionally at all. I was a pretty good trumpet player, but I'd say that I was a lousy piano player because I didn't follow through on it.

"My parents were very supportive in music. After I got into music, especially after I started studying trumpet, they were glad when I stopped practicing. To stop all the noise in the house, I think.

"I used to sell the *Saturday Evening Post, Ladies Home Journal* and *Country Gentleman* on a weekly basis. I used the money to buy a new bicycle, music scores and manuscript paper, and any other thing that I might have wanted that was within my budget.

Buddy, the trumpeter.

During those Depression years I tried to keep from adding an extra expense to my dad's tight budget. I also did a few unusual things during the summer months such as mowing the lawn for some neighbors, parking cars on the front lawn along the parade route when the circus came to town. There were other creative ideas that came along from time to time. I did these things through necessity rather than by desire."

When Buddy was a 16-year-old junior in Senior High School he drew a pencil sketch of President Roosevelt and sent it to him as a birthday present. It was one of many presidential sketches the young man drew for his teacher, Miss Bissett, who six months previously had begun her lesson plan on Lincoln. Buddy was inspired enough to attempt portraits of all the presidents, saving Roosevelt for delivery before his January 30th birthday. From Lincoln to Coolidge, the sketches, minus Roosevelt, hung on the classroom wall with pride.

On February 18, 1934 the Springfield paper ran an article about the event: the President had sent a Thank You letter in return. Buddy received it on February 17th. Buddy had had no formal art training, but the newspaper called his work "promising" as indeed it was. Up until a year previously he had done nothing but "lettering" but at that time began "comic sketches" which led to portraits. With Miss Bissett's encouragement, and the Presidential acknowledgement, Buddy found himself seriously considering a career in art. He immediately announced his intentions for taking an art class in his senior year of high school, then enrolling in the Kansas City art school.

"It was a decision for me when I younger," Buddy said, "whether I wanted to stay with the art world or really get into music. I decided on music because the lifespan on music is usually longer than art. Charlotte once and a while says, 'Why don't you draw anymore? Do some painting.' I just sort of lost interest in it."

Even in those early years Buddy lived for music. Another reason he switched to trumpet by the time he'd entered Pipkin Junior High was that he wanted to be in the school band, and enjoy some of the trips they took. He knew it would never be possible to lug a piano around, so, since he could already read music, he just had to learn how to blow that horn. He studied

Buddy and his parents.

under E.W. Peters for a few years, soon learning the rudiments of theory and harmony.

Around 1932 Buddy joined the famed Queen City Boy Scout Band. One of Buddy's favorite outings was when the Scouts took a trip to the 1933 Chicago World's Fair.

"I was in the largest Boy Scout band in the world, conducted by an old Scotsman called Richie Robertson. It was a 110-piece band. Big, big band, and a good band because at that time they were grading on primary, intermediate, and then concert band levels. Concert was the large one. But you had to go through the other two bands to be eligible to play in the big bands. We played concerts all over the place—St. Loius, Kansas City, Iowa, Illinois, all over. I was a Boy Scout. I got up to 1st Class, but that was about it. I think a lot of that was because I was good enough to be in the big band, the major band, and that helped. I was never into all that physical stuff that much: camping out, roughing it. I joined for the band. I'm camping out when I have to turn the blanket down to medium.

"We were always in band and orchestra contests. Usually we came out pretty much on top in all that. I got up to First Trumpet. I was in the group of firsts, and there were a lot of trumpets, 20 or 25. The Boy Scout band was all brass. In the orchestra I was playing Second Trumpet all the time; there we had 3 or 4 trumpets.

"Apart from the Boy Scouts, I was in both the band and orchestra (about 60 pieces) in high school. That band was conducted by Richie Robertson's son, James, who eventually became the conductor of the Springfield Symphony. After I got out of high school, I went into college and studied music there: theory and composition.

"In high school I'd already gotten a handle on writing high school type arrangements and I formed a little dance band. We got a job playing at a restaurant every Sunday—dinner music. It was a 12 or 14 piece band playing popular music of the day, early to mid to '30s. Usually we played ballads, or jazz music."

Buddy graduated from Springfield High School in 1935.

Being pretty good at baseball, art and music, his choice of career at this time was becoming difficult. He continued his education at Drury College and Southwest Bible College in Bolivar.

Graduating high school.

"When I went to Southwest Baptist [where he received his Doctor of Music degree], I studied orchestration along with theory and composition. I did a lot of studying on my own, too. After I did all that schooling I immediately got a job with one of the local radio stations because at that time it seemed like every radio station had a little band. KWTO—it's still there, with TV now, too. It was a popular band. We played a morning show, and sometimes in the evenings. Usually they were half hour shows. About 8 or 9 pieces of music. I played trumpet in the band and started writing for them, too."

He even toured as a professional trumpeter with several "territory" bands, traveling the Midwest region. This led to full-time road work as arranger—keeping orchestrations fresh for both audiences and the performers. From there he was asked to arrange music for other bands in the area and bands passing through, always on the lookout for able orchestrators.

"I had the help of my parents through college. They were supportive, but I don't know how proud they were because at that time people didn't think much of professional musicians because it wasn't a substantial life. But they never objected to it. It was a daily job, didn't pay much. I was still living at home, and the money I made wasn't enough to support anyone, even in those days, but it was a good experience."

It was at this point that Buddy developed his own system of constructing harmony, an element which always fascinated him. This intriguing system interested the great Nadia Boulanger (teacher of Elmer Bernstein, Aaron Copland and Quincy Jones). It was a poly chordal system, in which every tonic chord had its own scale.

He came up with it by studying what Stravinsky did. Prokofiev also used this system.

"I began using my arranging skills full blast through a contact in Springfield, a fellow I was studying arranging with privately. His name was Paul Mitchell. He was formerly the piano player

Buddy with Quincy Jones and Benny Carter at the 1998 Lifetime Achievement Award.

David Raksin, Elmer Bernstein and Buddy Baker.

with the Tommy Dorsey orchestra. And I met Joe Hanes who put together Rudy Vallee's orchestra and got Tommy Dorsey's band together. Paul and Joe were both from Springfield. So through those fellows I met other big band players. All the big bands at that time came through Springfield and I got to know a lot of the players. It was through those connections that I started making arrangements. They would suggest, 'Gee, this kid is doing some pretty good things, why don't you give him a shot at something?' And that came about a number of times. I did the full arrangements, and the big bands usually had a copyist who would make the parts. I did some of the parts at the radio station because we didn't have a copyist. I wasn't really paid well. Back then if you got $25 or $30 for an arrangement that was a whole lot for a pop song. Usually they wanted a record length, around 3 minutes on those."

CHAPTER 2
Young Man Goes West

The big band work began moving Buddy out west, which is where he began arranging music for radio programs: *The Bob Hope Show*, *The Eddie Cantor Show*, *The Standard Symphony Hour*, *Kay Kyser's Kollege of Musical Knowledge* and *The Jack Benny Program*. After three or four years on Jack Benny's show (working for Phil Harris), Buddy went on to work for Kay Kyser.

"When I first came to California I made a connection with Phil Harris through a bass player on the band I was arranging for. I started to do some arrangements for Phil. Then the Bob Crosby band, around 1939, 1940. The first arrangements I did for Phil were for his dance band. They were working nightly in a nightclub out here, and he was playing the *Jack Benny Show* on Sundays. I didn't do anything for Jack's show until after I was on the Bob Hope show. And I was never there on broadcast day because I was on the road with Bob Hope when we were doing Military bases around the country during World War ll.

"I loved Phil Harris. He was a free-wheeling, fun guy to be around. True, Phil didn't conduct the Benny show. It was conducted by Mahlon Merrick. But Phil was a bonafide star on the show with plenty of lines written into the script, and he did front the band on the opening number. I worked with Phil on and off the show since his band had a steady booking at the Wilshire Bowl nightclub and later at the Biltmore Bowl in the Biltmore Hotel in downtown Los Angeles. I also worked with him later at Disney on some animated feature that scrapped that sequence when they rewrote the screenplay.

"I didn't spend any time with Jack Benny. I hardly knew him, just a speaking acquaintance. I wasn't around the show that much. My only connection with that show was with Phil Harris. Jack didn't care who was writing the music as long as it sounded good for the show. It was different with the Hope show because I traveled with it.

"I got on the Bob Hope show through George Dugan who was the regular arranger on that. I became friendly with him, and he knew about my work, so when he got drafted, Skinnay Ennis hired me for Bob Hope's show on George's recommendation. By that time I'd got to know a number of the musicians on that show, so I wasn't with a bunch of strangers."

Buddy called in Xavier Cugat, and brought Stan Kenton into the program. Buddy and Stan formed a fast friendship that would later lead to Buddy's scoring Kenton's first nationwide hit, "And Her Tears Flowed Like Wine," which climbed into the top ten in 1944. Kenton and his orchestra took over the Hope show later, though when Kenton was stricken with an illness, Buddy took over until Stan was himself again.

As Buddy stated—quoted from in *Stan Kenton—Artistry in Rhythm* by William F. Lee: "One day at NBC in Hollywood, during rehearsal of an arrangement I'd done for Frances Langford, Stan stopped the band abruptly halfway through the introduction. He began to scrutinize the score carefully. Anxiously, I asked what the matter was. In his resonant voice, he boomed, 'Any time you can write louder than I can, I want to know what you did!' Besides being a great guy, Stan had a 'kinky' sense of humor."

During those wartime years, the network would tape Hope's shows during the Fall and Winter so that Hope could then rush off to entertain the troops. The show he took on the road was almost self-running, so Buddy wasn't needed for the overseas gigs. But he was there for some of the American ones.

"I worked with Bob Hope around 1941-1943, during the war. We always ate like the brass in the army, so we weren't really rationed. They took good care of their entertainment for the troops.

"Bob was great at ad-libbing. I saw him throw the whole script out into the audience one night. We were on the air! He was never at a loss for words.

"I stayed with the band guys mostly. Occasionally Bob would sit with us because he enjoyed being around musicians. During the shows he always wanted the GI's to sit down front instead of the brass because they don't yell or clap or anything. Sometimes Bob would sing, but mainly something he already had an arrangement for. I never did any arrangements for him. I arranged for Frances Langford, and once in a while Jerry Colonna if he had a comedy song, and some of the guest stars.

"So I got to know Bob and Frances quite well, and Barbara Jo Allen, and Vera Vague and Jerry Colonna. I think there were 10 writers that traveled with us. About 25 or 30 people total. I believe there were 17 in the band. We were sponsored by Pepsodent Toothpaste at the time. The show was so large that when we were doing the Army bases, it took two airplanes to take all the show and equipment. I believe we were flying from New York to Florida once and while we were over South Carolina, we got into a lightning storm, and the plane got hit by lightning. Another time we landed in Chicago and the runway was ice covered and we skidded off the runway.

"Kay Kyser and his *Kollege of Musical Knowledge* had a good band. I worked on that for two or three years. I did a lot of arrangements for his wife Georgia Carroll. I conducted the show most of the time because Kay Kyser wasn't a musician at all, but he had a good gift of the gab. I conducted all the numbers except a few. You don't have to be a rocket scientist to conduct a band when you've got a good drummer. That's the metronome back there.

"Then I worked a year on the *Eddie Cantor Show,* around the mid-1940s. He was a champion at being cheap. I remember one

Christmas Eddie brought in two turkeys and raffled off them off to the band as a Christmas present. I was doing mainly arrangements for guests on that show. Leonard Sues was the band leader. I never heard of him before or after the *Eddie Cantor Show*. He was a good trumpet player. One year was enough on that show. I also worked with Dick Stabile on *The Dean Martin-Jerry Lewis Show*. Nelson Riddle and I were the arrangers.

"After the Kay Kyser show, I got with Exclusive Records for the next three or four years. That company was owned by Leon Rene who wrote 'Sleepytime Down South' and 'When the Swallows Come Back to Capistrano.' After that I did a lot of recording with singers and good sized orchestras. I did one with Hal Kratzsch

who was one of the Four Freshmen and that session was sponsored by Stan Kenton. I don't think that record did too well. I don't think Hal went too far on his own. Later I heard that they rereleased that album and it was pretty good. Stan and I were very good friends apart from working well together.

"I did some work with Frances Wayne at Exclusive. She was originally with the Woody Herman band. Her big number was 'Happiness is a Thing Called Joe' (1945) with Woody Herman. At that time you couldn't rerecord the same arrangement on the same label for seven years. So seven years later I re-recorded the same arrangement with Neal Hefti, Woody's trumpeter. Neil has been my close friend for many years.

"I more or less ran all the sessions for Exclusive, whether it was my date or not. I had my own office there and worked there every day. We sort of pioneered doing these large orchestras on records because prior to that it was either a dance band type orchestra or groups. And I started using some of these bigger 30, 35 piece orchestras. You could always put a good, good group together, especially here in Los Angeles. All the studios used to have their own staff orchestras. Then the union broke that up—the quota system—so that other people would have an opportunity to work in the studio. But it really didn't change anything very much because all of our regular people then became first call people, and we always called the same orchestra back. That happened with all the studios here.

"I was widely known in the business. I worked with so many musicians, and they liked to work my dates because I had a lot of respect for them; whereas some guys would have a tendency to get a little rough with musicians, talk a little rough to them. But that's exactly the way to get the least out of them. I loved to chew the fat with them."

Buddy worked on an album called *Stars Fell on Alabama*, a collection of "star" tunes. He also put together the popular *Two in Love* album for the Verve label. The essay on the back of *Love* begins: "Under the baton of Buddy Baker, there are two orchestras heard here, each of 22 pieces; one is all strings, with flute and percussion, while the other is all woodwinds with valve trombone and percussion."

"In the strings and flute combo," recalled Buddy, "the flute player was George Poole, a fine studio player during those days. The woodwind combo included Willie Schwartz, the clarinet lead with the Glenn Miller band, and Willie Smith, the great lead alto with Harry James. The valve trombone player was Duke Ellington's Juan Tizol. Lou Bellson wrote the tunes and I did the arrangements. It was recorded for Norman Granz at Radio Recorders Studio in Hollywood. Compared to the junk that's out there today I think it still sounds pretty good."

It was Buddy's first opportunity to work on an album with his best friend, the already-legendary drummer Louis Bellson, who had performed and recorded with just about everyone: Ted Fio Rito (1941/46), Benny Goodman (and in the 1942 film with Peggy Lee, *The Power Girl*), Tommy Dorsey (1947-50), Harry James, Count Basie, Duke Ellington (1951-53), Red Norvo and others. He married singer Pearl Bailey in 1952 and served as her musical director for many years. Buddy also did musical arrangements for Pearl Bailey, for about 12 years. Her radio show was the last radio series Buddy worked on before getting into motion picture scoring.

"He's a warm, wonderful person," Buddy said. "I always say he's my brother, but I couldn't have had a blood brother that I love more than I love Lou."

Charlotte Baker added, "Buddy and Lou Bellson are like brothers. Louie always calls Buddy 'his teacher.' Now, he never defines that, so when they go places where they don't know him, they probably think that Buddy is a drummer. But he means composition. He studied with Buddy for years. He heard something of Buddy's many years ago; he said he was walking on Vine St. and he was talking with somebody, and he said, 'I just heard the greatest arrangement, with beautiful fiddles.' Louie said, 'Do you happen to know who did that?' And the man he was with said, 'Yeah, it's a young guy named Buddy Baker.' And Lou said, 'Well, I have to meet him,' and the friend said, 'Well, I know him.' And that's how they met. That was in the early 1940s, and they've been good friends ever since. He has a condominium in Sherman Oaks that's within walking distance of here. They also live up in San Jose when he's not traveling; he's still on the road a lot."

"One night," Buddy said, "Lou and I met Tony Bennett at Spago Restaurant, a celebrity hangout in West Hollywood. As we were leaving the place, of course the media people were there. They readily recognized Tony and some knew Lou, but none knew me. So they asked, 'Who are you?' I replied, 'I'm the godfather.' I thought that was an appropriate answer for being there with two well-known Italians.

"Lou Bellson is, in my opinion, the greatest Big Band drummer of all time. He and the late great Buddy Rich have been the standard bearers of fine percussionists for all drummers. He is not in excellent health at this time but he's still playing concerts, teaching and writing music for large college concert productions."

CHAPTER 3
Wicked Woman

In 1950 Buddy married Betty Jane Phillips. She was born in Birmingham, Alabama where she had her own local radio show at age fourteen, and sang with the big bands. In 1944 she represented Alabama in the Miss America contest where she soon caught the eye of Mickey Rooney. They married that year and divorced five years later. In 1950 she married Buddy and they divorced in 1957. And from 1961 to 1980 she was married to guitarist Barney Kessel. Oddly, even though her marriage to Kessel was the longest, and last, she kept her Baker name for the rest of her life.

She did some voices for cartoons and was a regular on television variety shows, such as those hosted by Dean Martin and Judy Garland. But her main fame came as a backup singer on some important songs: "I Can't Help Falling in Love With You" by Elvis Presley, "You've Lost That Lovin' Feeling" by the Righteous Brothers, "Dream Lover" by Bobby Darin, "That's Life" by Frank Sinatra, "You Send Me" by Sam Cooke, "Stagger Lee" by Lloyd Price, "Baby Workout" by Jackie Wilson, and others. She also dubbed vocals for films, her most famous session being the voice of Nancy Kwan singing "I Enjoy Being a Girl" in *Flower Drum Song*.

She died of a stroke in Rancho Mirage, California on April 2, 2002. She had two sons with Rooney, and a daughter, Cici, with Buddy.

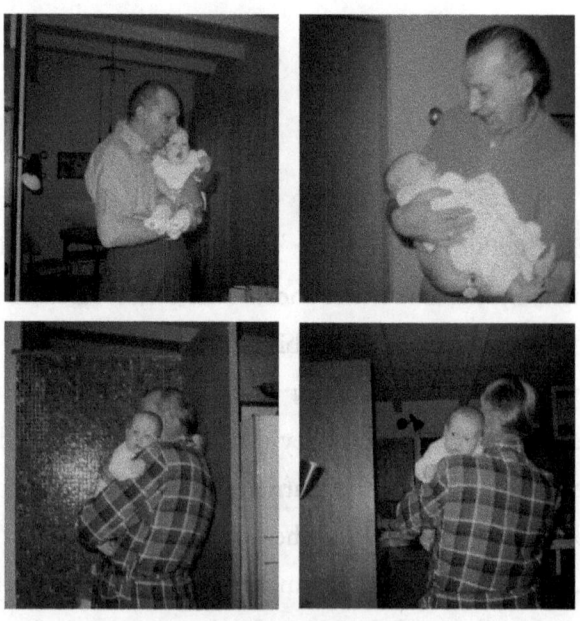

Buddy and little Cici.

"She got involved with one of these religious cults and she left Buddy," recalled Noreene. "It was one of those sad situations. They seemed to have a good marriage. She was beautiful, statuesque. Up until two years ago I'd heard from her every Christmas. I was very fond of her."

Growing up as a youngster during the studio system that produced classic films and scores, Buddy was most impressed by the works of Franz Waxman, Victor Young and Erich Wolfgang Korngold. During his composition work in the late 1940s Buddy began to devise his own harmony system which he continued to use and teach for the rest of his career. He also tried to get his composition style published.

"I haven't had time to set this down as an audio program," Buddy said, "and I'm very discouraged with publishers. I think that's a big waste of time for me. They always ask ridiculous questions and want you to do ridiculous things. The last thing I had going, I had turned in about 250 pages and they said, 'Well, we really expected 375 pages.' And I said, 'Well, what do I do? Write a bunch of ands and buts for you?' Basically it was our program at USC. It was a whole book on film music. It was one of the top publishers, too, but I don't want to mention their name because I want to get my script back from them. I never even got that back.

"George Bruns studied arranging and harmony with me. My harmony system was based on the fact that every type of chord has its own scale, which enables me to write polychordal instead of polyphonic. It's a little difficult to explain over the telephone. You need quite a study of harmony before you even touch this. I mainly put my private students on this. At UCS we really don't have time to get into that part of it, we're into more of the mechanics and the technical end of writing motion pictures, because they're supposed to have all their studies of harmony done before they get to us. It's a graduate program. My harmony teaching is sort of a one-on-one type thing."

After the war, Buddy began teaching orchestration at Los Angeles City College. Jerry Goldsmith, later-Oscar-winning composer of *The Omen*, *Patton* and *Planet of the Apes*, was in his first class. He also kept busy arranging for various orchestras

Buddy and Jerry Goldsmith.

and singers: Harry James, Stan Kenton, Kay Kyser, Glen Gray and the Casa Loma Orchestra, Bob Crosby, Phil Harris, Jack Teagarden, and Charlie Barnet. George Bruns, Barney Kessel and Harry James were a few of his private students.

"They were studying my harmony system and the whole thing. They would come to my home in Van Nuys, California. Classes lasted about an hour, though I didn't have a set time on it. It could be one and a half or two hours. I charged around $75 or $100 an hour. Harry James paid me a good price for the arrangements I made for the band, so it was kind of a trade-off."

Buddy at home.

Buddy also started a big 30-piece ensemble at City College, a full symphony with woodwind section plus six saxophones, four horns, harp and string bass. "It was a nice sound. The reason I started that was we wanted to start a rehearsal orchestra but we couldn't find enough string players. The older string players were in the studio and they wouldn't come out and do a rehearsal orchestra. So I said, well we just won't use strings. It was a good vehicle for all my friends who wanted to write and experiment with music. So I had several guys writing for it. They were fun to do. We did half a dozen or more concerts, but there was no schedule set for it."

Through his growing connections to the film industry, Buddy was now ready to try a movie himself. His first film was the independent feature (released through United Artists) *Wicked Woman* in 1953. The highly jazz-focused score featured two songs by Buddy and Joe Mullendore: "One Night in Acapulco" and the title song, "Wicked Woman," the latter sung by Herb Jeffries. "I did two or three independent films. The indie films—they were casual calls. One was called *Wicked Woman* with Beverly Michaels and Richard Eagen. They spent a lot of money on it, and used a good sized orchestra. It was blues oriented. The theme used for the wicked woman was always played on alto saxophone.

"Joe Mullendore was from Philadelphia. He was a fine film composer who later orchestrated *The Shaggy Dog*, and wrote the *Honey West* TV show theme. He was the first one to help me learn something about film music. I had landed the contract to do *Wicked Woman* and I was wise enough to get someone who knew the 'ropes' about films and film music to help me. At that time I had more 'guts' than brains but I was smart enough to get help from an expert who knew exactly what to do.

"I chose Joe to help and that formed an alliance that lasted until his death in 1990. I was able to get Joe on some Disney TV projects in the '70s. He was one of the 'regulars' with Four Star Productions in the '70s. He was adept at lyrics, but first he was a complete musician with the tools to do it all."

Wicked Woman, *1953*.

The *Wicked Woman* plot follows voluptuous blonde Billie Nash (Beverly Michaels) who has just bused into a small town to make a fresh start. The man magnet soon attracts a neighbor in her boarding house, Charlie Borg (Percy Helton), and uses him for money for the promise of a date; but her heart is really set on the owner of the bar where she was hired to be a waitress. It doesn't bother her that Matt Bannister (Richard Egan) is already married. She seduces him and he becomes so obsessed with the vixen that he agrees to sell the bar and run away with her to Mexico. The trouble comes when the bank requires his wife's signature to sell the place, so Billie impersonates her, but is informed that there's a four-day wait until the check can be issued. While waiting it out, Charlie discovers the subterfuge and threatens to tell Matt's wife the whole story unless Billie is "nice" to him. Matt catches the couple being "nice" and everything is ruined. Billie attacks Charlie, Matt confesses all to his wife, and Billie buys a one-way bus ticket to Kansas City, ready to start all over yet again.

The film's original title was *Free and Easy* and went through several rewrites to get its heated plot through the censors. Though that didn't stop it from being banned by the censor board in Memphis.

"*Wicked Woman* was a pretty good picture," Buddy said. "During the writing of the score of it, my father passed away and I had to go back to Missouri to be with my family during that sad occasion. For the two weeks that I was in Missouri, my old friend, Herschel Gilbert filled in for me and helped Joe continue with the *Wicked Woman* score. Herschel was musical director of 4 Star Television and was Joe's boss over there. Herschel, who later worked on *Gilligan's Island, Rawhide* and a lot of things, only did very few cues for *Wicked Woman*. It's not unusual for a composer to fill in for a fellow composer in case of emergency without asking for screen credit.

Wicked Woman, *1953*.

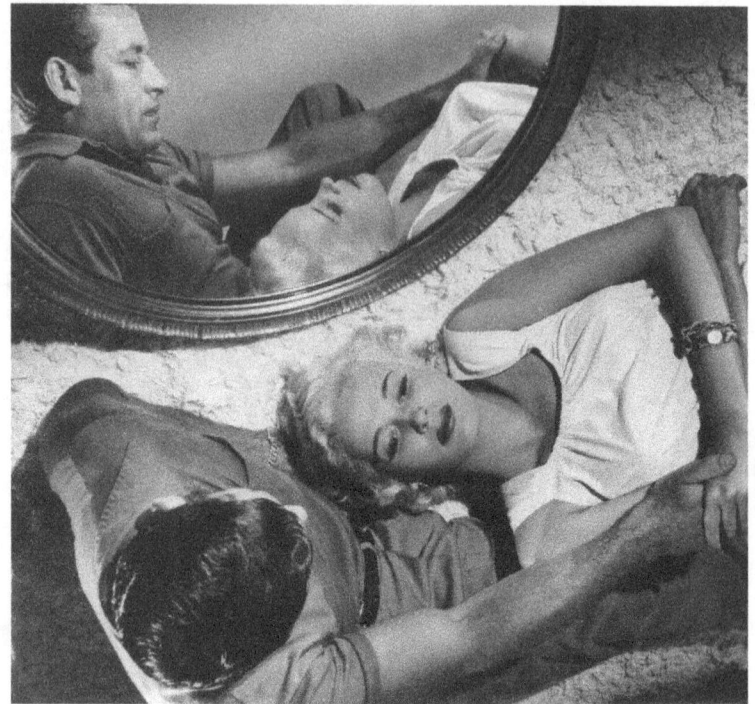

Wicked Woman, *1953*.

"I have helped, without credit, other Disney composers when they were in a pinch. I have had others composers jump in and help me when a real crunch was on. They never asked for a credit.

"Also around this time, before Disney, I did some local and regional commercials in the Los Angeles area. It was more or less a stop-gap solution to an early dry period for me. I'm at a loss to remember those commercials, but I recall one was for an auto painting chain. I can't remember any details except I was working with Maurice Hart, a morning radio host, who wrote the lyrics. He also made the contacts for the jobs through his many connections with the ad people."

Such connections would lead Buddy far.

CHAPTER 4
Scoring Disney

"George Bruns was my student," Buddy recalled, "and he got a job at Disney through Ward Kimball who was one of the 9 Old [animation] Men of Disney, and who had the Firehouse Five, a band of Dixieland players at Disney. Kimball was an off-the-wall, creative kind of guy. Stan Freberg used George on a lot of his commercials. George was out and out jazz, and Dixie trained. I worked with him on orchestrations and arranging. Apart from being a fine tuba player he was a great string bass player. He played great trombone, too. And he was a master cabinet maker. George started playing tuba with the Firehouse Five and Kimball found out that he was doing a little writing for a small animation studio here. I think it was UPA. Ward said to George, 'Well, since you know something about animation, why don't you come to Disney? Let me get you an appointment.' And Kimball got him into Disney. George called me to help him out after he'd only been there about six months. He asked me if I could come out there and work with him for a couple of weeks. So I went out there and stayed 29 years."

George Bruns is perhaps best known as the composer (with clever lyrics from X. Atencio) of "Yo Ho, Yo Ho, a Pirate's Life for Me" which still plays through *Pirates of the Caribbean* in the various Disneylands and Disneyworld. He also penned music for The Enchanted Tiki Room, The Country Bear Jamboree, the *Davy Crockett* TV series, and the catchy theme/score to the #1 film of 1969, *The Love Bug*. Of his work at Disney, Bruns sagely commented that Walt himself "thought of music as a supporting actor—it supports the picture."

"I first met George," said Buddy, "when he was playing bass with a local band, Jack Dunn's band, in the Zenda Ballroom in Los Angeles. Jack was a good friend of mine and I made some arrangements for him. George was trying to get started as an arranger himself, and he wanted to study with me. And you know the rest.

"A few months in at Disney, George was starting on *Davy Crockett*. He wrote that theme tune. I helped him on all those Crockett episodes. Then the original *Mickey Mouse Club* started about that time. George was supposed to do it but he was too busy doing the new *Disneyland* television show and had a few pictures to do, too. So they asked me if I could stay on and do the original *Mickey Mouse Club*. I was music director of that for the first three years. Five days a week.

Buddy leads the Mickey Mouse Club *orchestra.*

"The first year we did all the music live on stage with the kids. I had two rehearsal pianists that came in and I taught them the songs and worked out little routines, because I had a lot of arranging to do for that show.

"Then at the end of the first year it dawned on me that at the end of every number, those kids would stand there with college yells and clapping and all that kinda stuff, and that was ending every tune we did. So I sort of convinced them that I'd like to pre-score the music and play it back, and the kids would mouth back to it. For the next year they agreed that that was the way to do it because with that I could put an ending on the music at the end of each number and the kids wouldn't be standing there at the end of each number clapping and yelling. So for the next two years, that's the way we did it.

"I believe they were doing dubbing on pictures long before we started it on television because even George Bruns, when he was doing the first *Disneyland* show, that was all pre-scored. They didn't do any of that live. So we weren't the first to do that, but it was early on in television days.

"On *Mickey Mouse Club* my two rehearsal pianists—Frank Marks & Roger something—would get a good workout. They would make little lead sheets of the routines the kids were going to do, and give them to me so I would know what to write for the orchestra which would fit what they were rehearsing. That first year I was on the set every day, five days a week because the band was live. For the second and third years I would go down to the set and see how everything worked, make sure the playbacks were fine and all that. That kept me pretty busy.

"Jimmie Dodd and his wife wrote most of the tunes. They were great for what they were. He really had a handle on what to do for these youthful kind of tunes.

"'We're the Mouseketeers, we want to say hello…' I wrote that tune. It's my arrangement and Tom Adair wrote the lyrics. The '80s *Mickey Mouse Club* they did was sort of a Las Vegas version of a kid's show. It wasn't designed like the original, just for kids, and they didn't do cute little tunes, cute little acts and things that young children like so much. It was almost for teenagers. It didn't do well either. I only saw it once or twice and I gave up on it because it wasn't like the original at all.

Buddy's promo shot.

"There were five of us out there at Disney and we created what was known throughout the business as the Disney Sound: Paul Smith, Ollie Wallis, Joe Dugan, George Bruns and me. What's funny is that none of those fellows ever worked at another studio other than Disney, because when you started with Disney you were there for life. And the funny part of it is, none of them wanted to work at another studio because we had everything we needed right there at Disney, so it was okay.

"Paul once told me he made more money playing the stock market than he ever did playing for Disney. I remember Walt got mad with him once, after he'd done the film score to *20,000 Leagues Under the Sea*—Paul didn't even bother to turn it into the Academy so they know it's out there. So it wasn't nominated for an Oscar, because Paul didn't care. I had the utmost respect for him. Two composers have always been my idols. Paul Smith, the number one composer over all the rest. And Victor Young.

"Paul was the greatest composer I ever knew. In my estimation he was up there above Steiner, Korngold, all of them. Paul Smith was a master. Nobody ever knew of him, but that didn't hurt his writing. And if you don't believe he could write a good music score, listen to *20,000 Leagues Under the Sea*. *The Living Desert*. *Waterbirds*. Great, great music. I learned from him just by observing more and more.

"From time to time he would ask me to do a little thing for him. I remember when he was working on *Swiss Family Robinson*, he said to me one day, 'I've gotta write a damn polka. I don't know what to do with it. Could you do it?' So I wrote the little polka that's playing in the Treehouse. I probably did better financially on that little 'Swisskapolka' than Paul did on the whole score, because that's been playing in Walt Disney World, Paris, Toyko, all over, for the past 40 years. I think he gave it to me because it was sort of out of his category. He wasn't too comfortable with pop music.

"Paul had two fine musician brothers. One was Art Smith, a fantastic reed player. He was our first flute player on our sessions at the studio. His brother, George, was a studio clarinetist and a member of the Disneyland Marching Band for many years. Art has passed on and George was killed in an accident about 4 or 5 years ago [around 1998].

"The many producers and directors at Disney would pick out one of the five of us they liked the best to do their music. I've had occasions when I was working on a picture and the director would wait for me to finish a picture to start on his, rather than give it to somebody else. A lot of them didn't care. There was an agreement there that everyone was satisfied with the group they had. In fact, one time Winston Hibler wanted to bring in Max Steiner to do a picture and Walt said, 'What's wrong with our own guys? No, you can't bring him in.' I think it was kind of an insult to Walt—he thought he handpicked all of us. If he didn't like you, you didn't last there very long."

Working on *The Mickey Mouse Club* was an enjoyable challenge that, as musical director, put Buddy in charge of every aspect of the show's music. He wouldn't necessarily write songs or do arrangements on every episode, but he put it all together: from choosing music to dealing with the director's choice of music to unifying the sound for the final broadcast so that all audio fit the visuals perfectly. "The musical director has to make it all fit together like a big jigsaw puzzle," he told *Springfield Magazine*.

He went to work daily at Disney's Burbank studios which covered an entire block of choice real estate, down the street from NBC studios. The main quarters moved from Hollywood to a three-story building built in 1941 and designed with wings so that in case of need it could be converted into a hospital for the then-starting World War II. It was here that War Department instructional films were produced, and where Buddy soon found himself as a permanent staff member.

Toby Tyler, or Ten Weeks with a Circus, *1960. Walt Disney Productions. All rights reserved.*

Toby Tyler, or Ten Weeks with a Circus, *1960. Walt Disney Productions. All rights reserved.*

His first feature film for Disney was *Toby Tyler, or Ten Weeks with a Circus*, a nostalgic flit back to simpler times about a young boy, Toby Tyler (Kevin Corcoran) who runs away from the cruel words of his uncle to join the circus. Life at the circus isn't perfect, but with a newfound monkey friend, Mr. Stubbs, and circus workers Ben Cotter and Sam Treat (Henry Calvin and Gene Sheldon, both regulars from Disney's *Zorro*), Toby finds happiness and a sense of purpose. He trains to take over for an injured bareback rider and rides in the spotlight by the film's end in front of his apologetic uncle and aunt.

The film was only a moderate success at the box office, but a hit with critics. *The New York Times* wrote, "The very smallness of the setting pulls the gallery of circus people into cozy focus…this little picture…shines from within, mildly but sweetly."

Buddy also worked on *Walt Disney's Wonderful World of Color* which exploded onto television sets in 1961. The effect was literally magical. As *Variety* raved, "The difference between color and black & white was never so forcefully demonstrated as on Sunday night's premiere of the new hour-long [show] on NBC-TV. Seldom has the spectrum been so handsomely or imaginatively tinted up or such prismatic razzmatazz executed so beautifully." They admitted that the first half of the show was no more than a demonstration for RCA and Kodak, and wondered what the many viewers with black and white sets thought of the entertainment, but "it was an altogether persuasive and imaginative documentation of the origins of color and the use of tint in creating moods. It was a perfect blending of showmanship and salesmanship." The series also required a lot of music, by all the Disney composers.

World of Color also introduced Disney's new icon for color, the intelligently scatterbrained Ludwig Von Drake (voiced by Paul Frees), and gave those who missed it at theatres a chance to marvel at the cleverness of the Oscar-nonminated short, *Donald Duck in Mathmagic Land*, which *Variety* again admitted "provided some enlightening and ingenious vignettes out of Disney's creative bag of sight and sound tricks." The score to *Mathmagic* remains one of Buddy's finest.

One of Buddy's most enduring Disney feature films was released in the summer of 1963. *Summer Magic*, starring Hayley Mills and Burl Ives, contained seven Sherman Brothers songs, including the hit (for Disney and Ives both), "The Ugly Bug Ball." Based on the 1911 Kate Douglas Wiggin novel *Mother Carey's Chickens* (filmed before by RKO in 1938), the plot follows the

Carey family, down on their luck, who move from their large home in Boston into a fix-'er-upper in the country. *Time* magazine flippantly wrote, "Kids may be lured into dark, cool caverns with promises of sugar-coated escapism—escape from the traumas of the Little League, respite from the tyranny of the report card, surcease from the torments of the tooth brace and the training bra."

In March the following year, Buddy scored the beautifully-filmed *A Tiger Walks*, based on Ian Niall's 1960 novel. It was the story of a mistreated circus tiger, Rajah, who escapes when the truck he's being transported in breaks down. When his sadistic trainer is found mauled to death in the woods, Sheriff Pete Williams (Brian Keith) sends in the National Guard to hunt Rajah down. But Pete's 12-year-old daughter Julie (Pamela Franklin) intervenes via a TV interview to say that when she was in the woods, in the tiger's path, he did nothing to her, that the tiger was mistreated and should be captured alive. Children all over the world respond to her plea, and with the help of circus assistant Ram Singh (Sabu), Rajah is captured alive and placed in the zoo with a mate and cubs.

Critics weren't too taken with the film which has failed to become a Disney classic—though it hasn't helped that this is one of the many older projects kept in the studio vault for years without a promoted airing. *Variety* thought "the Buena Vista release does not succeed in its bid for adult enjoyment, principally because the film's center of comic and dramatic gravity is synthetic and childish. But most kids will probably get a boot out of it." Regardless, Buddy's tightly dramatic score alternated between delightful and exciting.

Buddy and Kathy.

CHAPTER 5
Familyland, Disneyland

"On March 11, 1962 Dad married Kathryn Louise Gwin," says Cici Baker, "at Noreene's house in Springfield, Missouri. Mom was born on May 2, 1924 in Twin Falls, Idaho and died on December 5, 1996 in Toluca Lake, California. They met at the restaurant that my mother was the General Manager of called Gaby's in Toluca Lake. He used to frequent the restaurant as it was close to the studio and got to know her there.

"Eventually, Dad helped her buy the restaurant which she then renamed Paty's. (She/They named it Paty's due to the high cost of neon, so it was most cost effective at the time to simply change two letters in the existing Gaby's sign than to have new neon made.) She, with Dad's help, turned Paty's into a Los Angeles landmark and it is about to celebrate its 50th anniversary. The restaurant was sold after my mother's death in 1996. Dad was actually a contributor to some of the dishes on the menu–including his Italian dressing!

Buddy and Cici in their Glendale home.

"Their first home together was in Tujunga, California and they then moved to Glendale which is the house that I consider my childhood home. It was a terrific house for entertaining and my mother threw some fabulous affairs there for Dad, studio friends, etc. as it was during this period that he was nominated for most of his awards (Oscar/Grammys, etc.). Dad, as you know, was very close to Louis Bellson, and he and Pearl Bailey were frequent visitors to the house as were his Disney colleagues and their families.

The Bakers in their Glendale home.

"In those days Dad loved his sports cars, and he and Mom would often take off for jaunts in the hot red car of the moment!

They loved to travel and we were frequent travelers to Europe and throughout the U.S. They loved to dine out, not only to enjoy great food, but get ideas for the restaurant. He and Mom also bought a ranch in central California during their marriage. The idea was to have a country escape, and also to raise cattle, chickens and pigs for the restaurant. The ranch was a successful Alfalfa ranch and did indeed produce livestock that we used at the restaurant and also sold. Dad and I would often leave after work and school on Friday and drive late into the night to get to the ranch when Mom was spending a great deal of time there setting up the systems and managing the livestock. It was a great deal of fun for them at that time.

Buddy and Cici at Noreene's house.

"We then moved to Toluca Lake which was considerably closer to both the restaurant and the studio. We were living in that home when they divorced."

Buddy and Cathy's daughter, Cici, was born on March 4, 1964. "I just loved Cathy, Cici's mother," stated Noreene. "Bud had good taste in the women he had. Cathy operated the restaurant herself. Cathy went off with someone. Bud's not a fighter. Not someone with an ill will or an attitude. Many times Cathy told me the worst mistake she ever made was leaving Bud."

"My daughter lives up in Lake Tahoe," Buddy said. "I talk to her once a week maybe, but she's always on the move. She's in the business that sponsors vacations for outstanding employees of corporations. They'll send 2500 Sony people to Hawaii for a week's vacation. She sets up all those kinds of things."

The year Cici was born was also the year of one of Buddy's most popular films. *The Misadventures of Merlin Jones* starred Tommy Kirk as (as the Sherman Brothers title song goes) "the scrambled egghead, the campus kook," the brilliant Merlin Jones who finds himself in trouble for accidentally being able to read people's minds after his brain is "electrified" during one of his many screwball scientific experiments. When he overhears Judge Holmby (Leon Ames) thinking/plotting out a murder and jewel heist for a book he's writing, he informs the police who refuse to believe him. So, Merlin, with the aid of his dedicated girlfriend Jennifer (Annette Funicello), set to dig up the Judge's prize-winning garden full of rose bushes; Merlin knows the diamonds

The Misadventures of Merlin Jones, *1964. Walt Disney Productions. All rights reserved.*

are hidden in nutshells under one of them. The police finally arrive, and all is explained involving the Judge's literary secret.

The second half of the film follows Merlin as he helps the Judge work out the plot to his new book: a thief has been hypnotized into committing crimes, but his conscious mind has no notion of what he's doing, so he is emotionally innocent. Having become an instant expert on hypnotism, Merlin assures the Judge that an honest man can't be hypnotized into doing something against his own moral code. But when Merlin has the Judge steal a chimp from the school lab, the theory is proved wrong and the Judge, having no memory of what he's done, sentences Merlin to jail time when Merlin is caught trying to put the chimp back. Again, all is explained and the Judge now realizes that perhaps everyone has the capacity for a little dishonesty.

As if done as two hour *Wonderful World of Disney* shows strung together for theatrical release, the screen story was actually written for the big screen by popular Disney author Bill Walsh (*Mary Poppins, The Absent Minded Professor, The Love Bug*, etc.). Bob Brunner, composer of such classic Disney films as *That Darn Cat, Blackbeard's Ghost, Gus* and *The Computer Wore Tennis Shoes*, got his start orchestrating *Merlin Jones*. Buddy's old friend and future *Haunted Mansion* collaborator Xavier Atencio received "special titles" credit along with Bill Justice for the clever *Shaggy Dog*-type cartoon cut-out credits that gyrated to the beat of Annette's catchy title song.

Music historian and author of *Duke Ellington's Music for the Theatre*, John Franceschina, shares his notes on Buddy's style in the *Merlin* score:

> Very string-heavy restful music and transitional material using electronic music to punctuate brainwave sequences; very subtle musical underscore to the mind-reading sequence in the library. Music is used very melodramatically, to emphasize the emotional or psychological moments rather than to contrast them. Rock and roll idioms used as background music in the soda shop sequences to emphasize the youthful characters and a *Dragnet* style motif accompanies the police station sequences.

Brunner uses traditional orchestral colors: the oboe is used for pathos, brass for heroics, guitar for rock, etc.

The travel music is very light-hearted, highly reminiscent of Gershwin's "An American in Paris" while the search music at the Judge's house involves quick string figures and punctuations of character looks (takes). The lie detector scene is subtly underscored with vibraphone (an electronic instrument to accompany an electronic device). Vibes are used again in the hypnosis scene—this time to suggest a kind of other-worldly quality. In both cases, the vibes are used as a reinforcement of the inner mind of the characters. Digging up the roses is accompanied by ascending musical figures (again reinforcing the action of the film rather than contrasting it).

The inebriation music begins as comic with sober musical punctuations, and goes from light to confrontational when Merlin kisses the wrong pretty girl. In the underscore with the cat, the vibes appear again as Merlin considers hypnosis. When the cat is actually hypnotized, the vibes-heavy music is joined by string tremolos, and heroic motifs that reinforce the ennobling of the cat to chase after the dog. The chase is underscored by appropriately scherzo-like musical motifs.

The chimp is accompanied by light strings and woodwinds with punctuations for chimp nods of the head and other business. The hypnosis of the chimp is again accompanied by vibes and electronic effects suggesting the Theremin (an instrument used in Hitchcock's *Spellbound* to suggest psychological stuff).

Interestingly, Baker uses more and more music as more animals take part in the film. Since the animals have no lines, the music rather speaks for them—or helps them communicate to the audience.

Providing seamless transitions from scene to scene or location to location seems to be one of the chief functions of Baker's score. Going from the courtroom to the Judge's house is accompanied by an obvious driving motif than blends into a string underscore once we are in the Judge's house. The driving music propels us, the string music lets us settle.

When the Judge is hypnotized, we hear the same vibes motif accompanied by strings (which seem to be the instruments that define the Judge's house) and later by woodwinds (preparing for the underscore of the theft to follow). When the Judge leaves the house at 9:00, the strings accompany him, followed by the woodwinds for sneaking around (another typical use of orchestral color), and later adding trumpets with mutes and low brass (adding to the texture and dynamic of the sound as the event of the theft builds up dramatically).

Taking Stanley out of bed is accompanied by a descending musical line (the chimp has to climb down so the music echoes that shape) and taking the chimp back to the cage is underscored by a rhythmic and jaunty tune—especially effective in counterpointing the melodramatic strings that accompany the lab scene and the subsequent discovery by the police. The jaunty tune suggests that there is no problem (or at least no expectation of being caught) so that when a problem does arise, the music hasn't given away the plot but actually helps the audience feel the surprise that Merlin feels.

The Monkey's Uncle, *1965. Walt Disney Productions. All rights reserved.*

Baker uses a bit of "source music" in the courtroom sequence when Merlin hypnotizes the Judge by the Oriental method (tissue paper on comb-kazoo sound). When the chimp goes to the witness stand, he is accompanied by a bassoon; once again Baker uses the orchestra to speak for the animals. The bassoon is characteristically a light-hearted jovial instrument capable of lots of funny sounds so its use here keeps the movie feeling light-hearted.

Returning to the Judge's chambers (a moment of possible danger) is accompanied by the Dragnet motif, again providing a musical accompaniment in line with the dramatic mood of the film.

One very interesting observation: Baker makes no use of the title song in any of his underscore. It is as if the title song was written after, or at least independently, of all the other music in the film. I don't know what use Baker could have made of the title song (as mundane as it is) but it is an interesting omission.

Buddy: "Bob Brunner first came in as a guest on the *Mickey Mouse Club*, playing the Theremin. He was good. He's a good piano player and also plays good string bass. Then when he got a little older and the *Mickey Mouse Club* kids were in their teens, he wanted to get into films. I taught him how to use a movieola. He was a good orchestrator. Some of the things he wrote were very difficult. A lot of notes and a lot of expressions; they weren't always that easy to play. When he did my *Monkey's Uncle*, he used my sketches and didn't change anything. I never let an orchestrator start making changes for me.

"That's what I liked about Walter Sheets. He would take my sketches and in some cases make it sound better than what I had in the sketch, without changing notes or anything. I worked with

Walter for 25 or 26 years there. Walter was actually doing some rehearsal piano work on the original *Mickey Mouse Club*. I think that's where I first worked with him. I had three rehearsal pianists on that show. Frank Marks was one. Frank was a fine pianist and a good composer, from Cleveland. He used to work out of New York City on a nice jazz show. He moved to California and I was able to help him get settled with Disney. For a while he orchestrated some of my stuff. He got busy doing some television things. I don't think he ever did a feature picture. Roger Spiker was another rehearsal pianist, though Frank was the original one I had called in. Walter, maybe he wasn't a rehearsal pianist, but he was called in to orchestrate some of these things."

Buddy was the first to admit that a good orchestrator can make a good composer sound great. "You have to have a good orchestrator who can follow a sketch and who can orchestrate it so it sounds the best for ranges and voicings. After I left *The Mickey Mouse Club* I did some cartoons and Bobby Brunner orchestrated for me and a couple others. As I got busier Walter Sheets was with me 99% of the time. He orchestrated a couple things for Bobby Brunner later on, too. Bobby got into a kind of bad situation at the studio. There was some kind of a strike going on with one of the unions. I don't know what he said to the unions, but the studio didn't like it. And I don't think he did another picture after that."

Merlin Jones was enough of a hit (earning a very good $4 million in its domestic release) to spawn a sequel, *The Monkey's Uncle*, the next year, reuniting the original cast (with Walter Sheets orchestrating now that Brunner was busy on his own scores). This time, the Judge, an avid Midvale College football fan, pleads with

Merlin to help the players hike up their grades so they won't get kicked out of college. Merlin has since invented an "honest way to cheat" by sleep learning which he applies to two of the goofiest team members. They make it through their oral exams with good grades, even though they give the answers in Annette's voice, who recorded the records from which they sleep-learned their lessons.

The second half of the film stirs up the heated football debate again: Mr. Dearborne (Frank Faylen) has always hated football and now revels in the fact that he's located Mr. Astorbilt who will give the financially-troubled Midvale College a million dollars on the one condition that they abolish football there. Luckily, the Judge also comes across Darius Green III (Arthur O'Connell) who promises $10 million to the school if they can prove his granddaddy right: that man-powered flight is possible. Merlin tackles the problem, enlisting the usual two idiot football players for muscle, and invents a working device! Unfortunately, not only is it found that Green and Astorbilt are one and the same person, but also that he's a raving lunatic who has escaped from a mental home. No money for Midvale.

The hip title song, "The Monkey's Uncle," was written by the Sherman Brothers and sung by Annette and the Beach Boys. Buddy stated, "I always liked Tommy Kirk, wonderful guy. He was good at the smart, nerd parts."

Scoring films required a different way of thinking, one that happily exercised Buddy's scientific mind. He found that film was the purest measure of time, even more accurate than a clock. For a sound film, there are 24 frames a second passing through a projector. Rather than time his music by minutes and seconds,

Buddy found that the surest way of getting the exact music count right was to measure time in frames and score to that.

As George Bruns became more engrossed in assembling much of the music for Disneyland, he, and Walt Disney, gave Buddy most of the projects for the 1964 New York World's Fair, including *Great Moments with Mr. Lincoln*, *it's a small world*, and *Carousel of Progress*. From there, Buddy became a staple of the Theme Park unit. Buddy recalled that his first scoring of a Disneyland attraction was probably the original music for the *20,000 Leagues* ride.

The difficulty of putting music to a living, moving ride was an interesting problem for the film composer. For Buddy's first whole ride, *it's a small world*, Walt Disney wanted the Sherman Brothers' title song to play continuously, in different languages, as the ride

Buddy and the Sherman Brothers.

progressed. The synchronicity alone was more than a challenge, which Buddy likened to putting "five marching bands in a gymnasium and trying to figure out what tune they're playing." He finally came up with the concept of looping the song in one-minute segments that would keep repeating, timing the water boats carefully beforehand to make sure the acoustics would not let the ear hear the song in the next language before the current one faded.

Buddy: "George Bruns and I did most of the more pop things, things that they would use in the parks. Films that had songs in them, we did a lot of that. George and Ollie and Joe Dugan did more of the dramatic type things. George and I were pretty good at that, too, but usually the directors wanted us to do the more pop things when they had to have those. George originally did the *Pirates* ride. After he left there, they expanded it and did all new scenes for it. He did the *Country Bear Jamboree*, and I added to that as well. One that I didn't add anything to that George did was the *Tiki Room* which was the first show in Disneyland. George did a marvelous job on that.

"*it's a small world* was done for the World's Fair in New York in 1964 and it was brought back to Disneyland in 1965 or '66, somewhere in there, after the Fair. In the beginning, Bobby Herman who was a fine pianist here in town and a great arranger, he did most of the arrangements for small world for the Fair. Then they brought it back to Disneyland and added scenes to it. I composed new music for the ride, using a full orchestra in various international styles for the show, and for the big clock out in front. Then they expanded it some more in Florida and they added more scenes to it when they got it into Tokyo. All of those added scenes I did. Because George had already moved back up to Oregon. It doesn't make any difference in difficulty adding on to others' work, because I know how they did it. It was just a matter of capturing the mood of the new scenes.

"The advance time varied from show to show. I always like to get in on the project as early as possible. The show's format would determine the procedure used for the music. Sometimes it was like scoring a motion picture where the music comes last.

"I was in New York working on the '64 World's Fair when my mother passed on. It was on April 14th, 1964, the day that President Lincoln was shot in 1864 at Ford's Theatre in Washington 100 years earlier. She was 72 years of age."

Coincidentally, it was *Great Moments with Mr. Lincoln* that he was then working on. Originally also built for the New York World's Fair, *Lincoln* became the first Disney attraction, once it moved to Disneyland, to play on both coasts simultaneously. Buddy scored the entire show, pre-show included, using three of his usual orchestrators: Robert F. Brunner, Walter Sheets and Franklin Marks. Alan Davies was the choral arranger, adjusting the 32 voices at varying distances from the microphones in order to create a sense of depth and church-like majesty. Stereo was also used to highlight the style. Vocal tracks were added as the music progressed which lent a grandness to the dramatic subject, ending on a rousing "Amen."

Buddy adapted some of the themes he used in his *Johnny Shiloh* (1963) film score. "Soldiers of Liberty" became the *Lincoln* Theme—"North and South" became "Hail to the Flag." "Civil

War-horses," "Dixie" and "When This Cruel War Is Over" were also utilized.

Another attraction that had its origin at the 1965 World's Fair was *The Carousel of Progress*, a rotating animatronic stage show in which a typical American family is shown alongside the evolution of technology, to make living easier. Instead of the stage moving, the audience turns in this circular building. The Sherman Brothers again gave the theme song a positive spin, with the aptly named "There's a Great Big Beautiful Tomorrow," after Walt Disney scrapped the idea of using all historic songs. As the stage turns, the song undergoes its own transformation, into a new decade and a new style of arrangements. Ragtime, swing, lounge and more "modern" sounds follow the family's story as time marches on. Buddy's entrance music to the show was equally imaginative against the 10x40 foot Kaleidopohonic screen which showed guests the music in rainbow patterns of swirling colors as light echoed song and voice. The voice was Western star, Rex Allen, who originally recorded a complete version of the attraction in May of 1963 and returned later that year to finish the singing against Buddy's completed music tracks.

In 1967, after a second season at the World's Fair, *The Carousel of Progress* moved to Disneyland to become part of the all new Tomorrowland. Buddy wrote additional music for visitors to marvel at the wonders of Progress City, a 6,900 square foot model based on EPCOT's original concept, on the buidling's second level. When "There's a Great Big Beautiful Tomorrow" returned to Disneyland in 1998, Buddy scored yet more orchestral music for Tomorrowland's *Innoventions*, a showcase of hands-on technology that was housed in the old Carousel Theatre. The robotic Tom Morrow sang a new version of the theme, scored by Buddy, updated by the Sherman Brothers as well, called "There's a Bright New World of Innoventions."

When *The Carousel of Progress* left Disneyland after six years, *America Sings* was brought in to fill its theatre, and Buddy was back. With 114 Audio-Animatronic animals singing a flurry of American popular songs for 24 minutes, there was plenty to do. Every era of American music during the country's two centuries was represented, with 39 songs finally being chosen from hundreds.

Tied together with the iconic American tune, "Yankee Doodle Dandy," with five sets of lyrics written by Al Bertino, the project was narrated by Bald Eagle Sam, more commonly known as Burl Ives. The first scene contained "My Old Kentucky Home," "Single Girl," and the spirited "Down by the Riverside." The second act showcased America's expansion Westward, with "The Old Chisholm Trail," "Billy, the Bad Guy," and "Home on the Range." Scene three heard a lamenting mother rabbit asking "Where Is My Wandering Boy Tonight?" before a pig asked almost the same question with "Bill Bailey, Won't You Please Come Home?" Act four pushed into modern times with "Boo-Hoo" sung by kittens, ending with the very modern (at the time) "Joy to the World" via the Three Dog Night version.

A press preview was held when *American Sings* sang for the first time on June 29, 1974, treating guests to a sneak preview of the attraction's album which was soon to be released. The singing stopped on April 10, 1988, though many of the robotic characters still live on in the ever-popular *Song of the South* attraction, *Splash Mountain*.

The Tomorrowland revamp of 1967 also brought in one of Disneyland's most unappreciated and longest rides, the very singular WEDway PeopleMover. Its clean electric propulsion was yet another event aimed for the 1964 World's Fair, and was again scored by the master. Sponsor Goodyear requested that its catchy jingle, "Go, Go, Goodyear" (written by space-age pop writer, Bob Thompson) be the main theme in the ride's score. Buddy took the instructions and ran through marching bands, bongo beats, swinging jazz and many other styles to keep the ditty fresh and exciting on its journey through 1995, when the ride ceased to roll. The ride still delights (minus original score) would-be line-haters to this day in Disney World by giving them a long place to sit for a while.

When *The Swiss Family Robinson Treehouse* first opened in Disneyland in 1962, visitors were treated to a looping version of "Swisskapolka," as played by the pump organ from the film. Except during Christmas, when a medley of Christmas carols were played. In 1999, the attraction changed, as all must, it seems, to become *Tarzan's Treehouse*. But Buddy's music can still be heard on the Professor's scratchy 78 record ever turning in one of the rooms.

One of Buddy's most endearing and enduring musical treatments was arranging the Sherman Brothers' perfect children's musical trilogy, repackaged as a feature in 1977 as *The Many Adventures of Winnie the Pooh*. "Originally the three

Buddy and the Pooh *Oscar.*

Winnie the Pooh shorts were planned to be a feature picture," Buddy explained. "We started with *Winnie the Pooh and the Honey Tree* in 1966. At the time they'd just rereleased *The Wizard of Oz*, and I think Walt thought this isn't the time to release another feature out there and try to buck that thing. It was a big picture.

So that's when they divided *Pooh* up into three episodes. First they were sponsored by Sears and Robuck. They sold a whole lot of Winnie the Pooh dolls and stuff. I had to revise some of those cues to leave holes for commercials for television. At the same time I had laid out the shorts so they could put them all together so it would sound like one long film. We used to run into that a lot, when we had to do a TV version and a motion version for later because most of our TV versions here were released in Europe as feature pictures.

"The Sherman Brothers were great to work with. We first worked together on *Summer Magic*, then on the three *Winnie the Pooh* shorts, and probably a dozen projects through the years. They're fun to work with. They would've played their songs for Walt, and he would've said, 'Oh that's good. That'll do.' That was his way of saying you didn't need to change anything or add anything to it. I'm probably the only composer in this business who has never had anything thrown out. The Shermans and I get along just fine. I still work with them from time to time."

In 1999 *Mr. Toad's Wild Ride* was ousted in favor of *The Many Adventures of Winnie the Pooh* in Walt Disney World, followed the next year by a very different adventure in Tokyo Disneyland as *Pooh's Honey Hunt* (complete with bouncing Tigger room!). Buddy rescored music from the first two shorts for both parks, even using composer Richard M. Sherman as a kazoo player during the Heffalumps and Woozles sequence (as he did in the original cartoon).

On May 31, 1967 Buddy recorded 47 different cues of music

for *Adventures Thru Inner Space,* a Disneyland ride in which patrons were "shrunk" to the size of a molecule and led, like *Pirates*, into a strange new world—this time, inside the atom of a snowflake. As Paul Frees correctly narrated, "Although your body will shrink, your mind will expand." Inside your Atomobile you experienced many wondrous visuals, as well as Buddy's most ethereal Disney score yet. Using a bass marimba to give sound to a water molecule and an electronic flute to lead riders into thinking they are hearing a dash of frenzied molecules were only some of the more creative aspects of the tonal, experimental score. Eventually the Sherman Brothers popped in again (near the ride's end), this time with a not-so-experimental "Miracles from Molecules," an amusing march that had the vocal quality of their *Carousel of Progress* ride. The ride finally closed its doors in 1985, two years before the current space simulation, *Star Tours*, claimed the Disneyland area.

When Walt Disney died on December 15, 1966, it left a bottomless hole to fill in the Walt Disney Company. Buddy himself had a recurring dream for the next five years of meeting Walt at his home in Palm Springs. "I think all of us at the Studio felt that he was still there. Someone in a meeting would say, 'Well, Walt wants this.' And Walt was long gone. Until my last day at the studio, I always felt Walt was still there."

CHAPTER 6
The Haunted Mansion

What began as art sketches in 1951, what is now known and beloved as *The Haunted Mansion* today first began its pre-musical journey as the residence of Captain Bartholomew Gore, AKA Blackbeard. Originally intended as a walkthrough attraction, the gloriously eerie manor went through several manifestations by the time it finally opened in California in 1969. Walt Disney had set aside the *Mansion* work to get his four new attractions ready for the 1964 World's Fair. But it was the problem of continuous music in a walkthrough "museum" attraction that provided yet another stumbling block.

Thanks to the Omnimover system which premiered in Disneyland's recently remade Tomorrowland in 1967, giving *Adventures Thru Inner Space* a modern boost, audiences could now move slowly through the new *Haunted Mansion* ride in their Doom Buggies, soaking up all the details of playful fright, Paul Frees narration, and music.

© *Disney Music Publishing.*

First, though, there was the decision whether to make the *Mansion* scary, or funny. X Atencio wrote the show (as well as *Pirates of the Caribbean*), gathering elements from the long history of its different versions through the years, and also penned the lyrics to Buddy's most famous song, "Grim Grinning Ghosts." The short, minor-key tune is first heard before entering the dark elevator, where its creepy chords are emitted by silent film organist, Gaylord Carter. When Carter recorded the music, the resonance of the organ was so forceful, the microphone had to be moved into the studio's hallway in order to avoid its intense reverberation.

The sophistication of *The Haunted Mansion* required many one-minute loops synchronized in reference tempos which allowed its basic theme not to seem to overlap; this was one of the reasons Buddy wrote the theme in half notes, letting the music be more pliable at its slower pace. It also allowed the 4/4 tune a more haunting majesty. From the moody version playing on the organ in the foyer to the complex graveyard scene (the biggest set of the ride), it was a trick to score this moving entity while not overloading the audience on one motif.

To enhance mood and keep things lively and "deadly," Buddy also developed some innovative sound effects and backwards tape tracks, in collaboration with sound effects artist Jimmy MacDonald. For the graveyard scene, over 40 tracks were recorded in April of 1969, including one musician beginning at the end of the music and progressing towards the start so that when the tune was reversed and played back at normal speed, there was an odd instrumentation and breathy quality to it.

On hand for graveyard vocals were Ernie Newton, Bill Lee,

Bill Reeve and Betty Wand. The five singing busts—who also "appear" as ghostly faces on the busts—led by *Pirates* voice Thurl Ravenscroft, included Chuck Schroeder, Verne Rowe, Bob Ebright and Jay Meyer. The creepy crew also lent a final touch of harmony to the very end of the ride when Imagineer Leota Toombas asks us all to hurry back…and be sure and bring our death certificates.

And people were dying to get in. On August 9, 1969 over 82,000 guests set a record for the most guests in one day, in its very first week.

CHAPTER 7
After Walt

Working with Walt Disney himself was always a treat. Buddy admitted that the Man in Charge didn't know one note from another, but he knew what was right for every picture and ride that had his name stamped on it. Their minds were often the same when it came to music cues, which helped out Buddy greatly on the budget he could ask for. Because what Walt wanted, they got. You knew if Walt wasn't pleased with something—he had a way of tapping the arm of his chair which said "it's no good."

Walt could be gracious and there was never any conflict between the two men. Mainly because Buddy was smart enough to avoid the boss—if he could—when the front gate guard gave him the high sign (codename "bear suit") that Walt was in one of "those" grumpy bear moods. Those were the times to stay out of his way. Of course there were days when it was unavoidable; Buddy's parking space was only two spaces away from Walt's. And when the Boss was in a foul mood, the long sidewalk walk to the studio could become a long, long walk in silence.

In one instance, Walt wasn't happy with the score to a film, and called Buddy in to redo it. When Buddy told the company executive in charge of the film that he was going to need the same amount of time (8 weeks) as the original composer, the exec flipped out. "Eight weeks! That's impossible! The project is already sold!" Walt simply said, "Unsell it. Give him the time he needs to do it right."

"Most of the press was directed at Walt himself," said Buddy. "He employed the greatest animators in the world, but could you name one of them? The five composers there, including myself, I think were the greatest collection of composers working, but who knows about us? Walt always gave us credit for what we did, and we got screen credit, but no one ever picked up on that. We had probably more music there than at any other studio. Walt loved music."

Buddy was also good at sketching, but "I never told Walt about my artwork. He was a firm believer that too much talent in too many fields was not good. He thought, be the best you can in one field. We always talked about the music for the project that I was working on. It was always a mistake to try to get 'too close' to Walt. Sometimes we would talk about 'trains.' He was a railroad lover, especially for steam engines. One time I asked him about riding up through the Tehachapi Pass on a Diesel freight train. A friend of mine was the engineer on that route and had asked me if I'd like to go along for the ride. Walt said, 'I guess that's okay if you want to ride a GD street car.'

"One film I did called *Summer Magic* had a very fine arrangement by Bobby Hamilton. But he'd written in this little triangle into the score, so when Walt heard the whole thing he turned to me and said, 'Sounds great, but what's that telephone doing in there?' So, I re-recorded that section without the triangle and everything turned out fine."

Buddy found his boss to be very perceptive musically and soon learned his quirks in that direction and altered his scores in a way that would please him. Walt didn't care for high-piercing instruments, piccolos and often the high notes of a flute. Also, one way to ruin a dialogue scene in Walt's ears was to put double reed instruments in; Walt was afraid that if an oboe, English horn or bassoon were put behind the talk, they would steal the scene.

Buddy would never copy anyone. His sound was his own. He considered his greatest asset being able to move with the times. "We were sort of off on an island at Disney," he said. "There would be times when a whole year would pass and I wouldn't even go over the hill into Hollywood. I really enjoyed those times. But from a publicity standpoint it's not good because nobody ever hears of you. But I never really thought much about publicity because I was always doing what I liked to do anyway."

Walt Disney Studios loaned him out to WED (which stood for Walter Elias Disney, and was their code word for Walt Disney Imagineering) for extensive Theme Park work. It actually ended up as a longer gig than his film composing. Buddy acted as composer and consultant to Walt Disney World, EPCOT (Environmental Prototype Community of Tomorrow) and the international Disneylands to the end of his life. At one point he had been named Musical Director of WED Enterprises, scoring for every global Disneyland except EuroDisney in France.

"I've done 52 park attractions," he said. "In all those years I never had an agent. Because I had more work than I can do. I'm still keeping busy.

"It was too bad Eastern Airlines didn't survive the battle of the airlines. *If You Had Wings* was a fun show to do and X [Atencio] and I did enjoy working on it. Because I've been with the parks since their inception, we have developed special techniques and ideas that we know will work. Most shows take from six months to a year to do. Each show is different, though. Sometimes things must be rescored, or people recast." It might take half a year to find just the right band(s) for the needed sound or voices for characters.

Though Walt was gone, many of the projects that Walt himself planned would go on for years. Buddy worked on over 165 scores for Disney television and film. And he never seemed to take time off. Walt once asked him if he'd had his vacation yet, to which Buddy replied, "I haven't had time yet." Walt said that he had had his, so Buddy'd better take one too. "He ordered me to take a vacation, and the work would wait until I returned."

Walt was loyal to his employees, always using his staff composers rather than hiring outside the studio system—as is the only way today. Buddy said, "I probably learned more from Walt in the years I was there than I have ever learned from any formal education or any other means of broadening my scope. He was a great teacher."

The year after Walt's death gave Buddy one of his busiest and brightest scores. *The Gnome-Mobile* (1967), starring Walter Brennan and the *Mary Poppins* kids (Karen Dotrice and Rodney Winthrop), was based upon *The Gnomobile: a Gnice Gnew Gnarrative with Gnonsense, but Gnothing Gnaughty* by Upton Sinclair (1962). The story follows California lumber tycoon D.J. Mulrooney (Brennan) who, during a picnic in a redwood forest with his grandchildren, comes upon a two-foot high gnome named Jasper (Tom Lowell) who laments not being able to find a wife and tells of the danger that his species will become extinct because there are so few gnomes about. The big people happily take Jasper in their Rolls-Royce to locate other gnomes, but he's kidnapped by Horatio Quaxton (Sean McClory), seedy proprietor of "the Academy of Fantastic Freaks." Mulrooney orders his vice-president, Ralph Yarby (Richard Deacon), to conduct a search for the little person, but Ralph has the crazy old man promptly put away. With the aid of his grandchildren, Mulrooney is extracted from the sanitarium, Jasper is freed from Quaxton's evil show, and a manic chase over the mountains ends in the land of the 1100-year-old gnome king and his valley of pretty gnome maidens. A lengthy mating contest, beautifully, energetically underscored, has girls chasing Jasper through the brush, and the winner—the shy

Violet—gets to marry him. The delighted Mulrooney generously donates 50,000 acres of his land to the gnomes to insure that they will frolic here for all time.

"The Gnome-Mobile" title song was another catchy Sherman Brothers romp, sung with vigor by the three main characters in their gnome-filled vehicle.

Buddy again worked with Walter Brennan the following year on the even more musical, *The One and Only, Genuine, Original Family Band*. But as the composer recalled: "Walter Brennan could carry a tune for about two bars but then it would be off. I remember working with him two bars at a time to get a song complete. In the mornings when we would meet on stage, he was always the first one there. He really worked hard at it. Eventually we got a decent track out of it.

"There was one scene where the Family Band was marching down the street and what they had put in the score sounded like the United States Marine Band, not like a five-piece band. I remember I took the picture, checked out the tempo and we wrote something in there that sounded sort of out of tune, like a little country band, to make it seem real. That's all I had to do with that show."

His next film, *Rascal*, released on June 11, 1969, tells the beautiful story of a boy (Billy Mumy) and his pet Rascal, a raccoon he saves from the clutches of a lynx in the year 1918 in the little town of Brailsford Junction, Wisconsin. Of course often Rascal gets into mischief, and is nearly killed by the lynx a second time, and is finally released back into the wild when a female raccoon comes along. The 85-minute film showed off what Disney—and Buddy—did best when it came to scripted real-life adventures.

King of the Grizzlies (1970) was based on the novel *The Biography of a Grizzly* by Ernest Thompson Seton (1903) and was filmed on location along the Canadian Rockies in Alberta and British Columbia, in Banff National Park, Kananaskis Forest, Yoho National Park and in the Stoney Indian Reservation. It is the honorable story of Moki (John Yesno), a Cree Indian working as a foreman on a ranch in the late 19th century West, who develops a special bond with a bear cub who escapes his rifle fire. Discovering that it has only four toes, Moki names him Wahb, which means four-toed grizzly. As the years pass, the two come in contact with each other more and begin to respect their ways.

The film opened as a double feature with the re-released *Sleeping Beauty*, enticing *The New York Times* to write that it "should be a delight for cub scouts of all ages."

"I don't watch much," Buddy admitted. "I don't listen to much of my own stuff. I watch the original *Mickey Mouse Club* almost every week because one of the pictures I did runs along with that show late at night. I did a lot of those nature things. I look at that every once and while to check and see I'm getting my ASCAP credit. It winds down yearly. You have to watch them and make sure they're recording everything, keeping up to date with it. I get more on that than I get for doing the show; I get composer's credit for the *Club* song as well, not just for the instrumental cues. It's been published by Walt Disney Music." He later received two Grammy nominations for *The Electric Company* album (1973), and *America Sings* (1974), based on the Disney attraction and featuring Burl Ives.

Possibly Buddy's most popular film came in 1975 with the big western hit, *The Apple Dumpling Gang*. Composer John Franceschina again gives musical notes on Buddy's work:

> Baker creates a Western sound emphasizing harmonica and guitar and a folk-like melody. He incorporates strings as a melodramatic effect (not unlike Merlin Jones). After the opening card game, the music gets very lively with rapid banjo figures and lively string runs and the melody in the brass. Seems as if Buddy is trying to propel energy into the film at the very top.

The Apple Dumpling Gang, *Walt Disney Pictures*, 1975. Copyright Walt Disney Productions.

As in *Merlin Jones,* the music is essentially transitional, getting from one scene to another, one place to another, and mood setting, using harmonica, guitar, and strings (the chief sounds of the musical palette) to underscore sentiment (especially where the kids are involved). Ethnicity is also accompanied in the music with the Chinese motifs and the comedians in the film are appropriately accompanied by comic music (the firehouse scene is especially cleverly underscored).

Unlike in *Merlin*, Buddy makes good use of the title tune throughout the film, creating atmospheric music for the kids at the mine (for example) or the trip in the mine car. The orchestral palette also includes celesta (kind of an analogue to the vibes in *Merlin Jones*) and "source music" for violin and piano in the restaurant to suggest the old west. Baker uses a lot of motifs in the film as well as the title tune: a "mysterious mine" motif, "gold" music, and the "Here Comes the Bride" motif (see discussion below) are examples of this. In the last example, he cleverly rephrases known music to accompany the dramatic situation: during the discussion of marrying Dusty, Baker uses a subtle suggestion of "Here Comes the Bride" in the underscore—disguised enough not to be flagrant, but familiar enough to be effective. The same "Here Comes the Bride" motif reappears as the group moves to the barbershop for the wedding. Not only does Baker provide a subtle connection to a known musical phrase, he also connects the dramatic moments together through the use of musical motifs.

The Apple Dumpling Gang, *Walt Disney Pictures,* 1975.
Copyright Walt Disney Productions.

Whether or not Buddy intended this, the use of brass music to accompany the fight over the brass bed is very clever (along the lines of the "Here Comes the Bride" musical joke) and the use of the barroom

The Apple Dumpling Gang, *Walt Disney Pictures*, 1975. Copyright Walt Disney Productions.

tack piano to underscore the actual fight evokes Matt Sennett silent film routines while being absolutely appropriate to the Western tone and flavor of the film.

The chase after the kids uses the rapid banjo figures again and the trumpet heroic fanfare evokes The Light Cavalry Overture, a famous melodramatic work by Franz von Suppe. What's particularly praiseworthy about this score is that it develops out of everything we hear in the first minutes of the film. The rapid banjo figures, the harmonica, guitar, strings, and brass are presented in ways that are idiomatic to the Western sound at the very beginning of the film and then throughout the film. Baker seems to deconstruct that sound, using this or that color to evoke the proper sentiment. Nothing seems out of place and the entire film score is unified within the tone and tune of the title song.

Perhaps Buddy's biggest, and possibly only bias for musical scoring was that the music should blend in completely, not overwhelm, the visuals. He thoroughly believed that no one was coming to the movies to listen to the score, be it Buddy Baker or John Williams. Concerts were where you listened to music, not films; if you find yourself listening to the music and not paying attention to the story, there's something wrong. He likened film composers to writers of literature rather than music, since "we are not writing music for our own entertainment. The music must blend with the film, as a single ingredient in a recipe. A chef doesn't like a particular seasoning to stand out in one of his concoctions. He must hit upon exactly the right proportions to make the taste total, unfragmented. The same holds true for composers. Music has to fit like a proverbial glove because it has to complement so many factors: story, atmosphere, action."

Some, like lifelong friend David Raksin (perhaps best known as the composer of *Laura*), disagreed with the "invisible score" theory. Buddy felt that the most important way of scoring a picture was to discover the film's own tempo, and really understand the concept of framing the film. "Get a dramatic sense of the picture."

He didn't care for synthesizers unto themselves, or as replicating machines, though he did think them wonderful instruments when used as an added section to the orchestra. "Machines don't have heart, and that is the difference."

CHAPTER 8
Third Time Charm

Buddy's marriage to Charlotte Baker around *The Apple Dumpling Gang* time was the relationship that lasted him rest of his life.

"I was born in March 27, 1920 in San Diego, California," says Charlotte. "On October 16, 1976 I married Buddy. My grandparents on my father's side came from Denmark. I was very used to growing up with an accent around. So when Buddy and I have traveled, it always seems easier for me to understand people from different countries. On my father's side, they were very artistic, they played musical instruments, they were artists. My grandfather's father was something called Seventh in Line of Service to the King of Denmark. On my mother's side, they were all very practical: Judges and circuit writing and Baptist ministers. I studied classical piano for five years when I was a kid, but then as I got older I wanted to play pop music, and I had gotten so used to reading what was on the page that I couldn't improvise. It was very debilitating to me, so I gave it up.

"I worked for the granddaddy of all disc jockeys, Al Jarvis. He started a program called *The Make Believe Ballroom*. In 1940 I heard him say on the radio that his secretary was sick and he was way behind on getting his letters out and all that, and anybody who would like to help, come on down to the studio tomorrow. I thought, 'My gosh, there's going to be a line around the block.' But there were two other girls apart from myself. I just wanted in the worst way to get that job, because this was in the time when the big bands were so popular. I was just a big band junkie. I got the job and I was so thrilled because I got to meet a lot of band leaders and singers like Frank Sinatra. Then I got into music publishing, and I worked for artists who had their own music publishing companies, like Johnny Mercer and Peggy Lee. Gene Autry had seven publishing companies for which I did all the administrating (contracts, the royalties, the licensing, all that sort of thing). And Rod McKuen. I worked for him for ten years.

"I met Buddy in 1946. My ex-husband introduced us. And then I didn't run into him for another year, 1947, and by that time I was divorced, and I was working for another disc jockey over at radio station KFWB in Hollywood. Martin Block, who was very famous in New York, came out to California and heard Al's program, *The Make Believe Ballroom*, and took the title and went back to New York and made a fortune, whereas Al kind of piddled along. Actually when I started working for Al, he had a show called *The Football Widows and Widowers Club*. It was a Saturday program of course, and people sent in photographs, snapshots, and I would cut them out and paste them on a membership card and collect their dimes. I got paid $30 a week in dimes.

Buddy and Charlotte at an awards banquet.

"Then I had gone back to work for a disc jockey who came out from New York who had been Martin Block's substitute when he was off. His name was Maurice Hart and I did an early morning show with him on KFWB. The owner of KFWB was very philanthropic minded, and he gave a kind of a big bash there on the lot. Buddy had come over to conduct for Herb Jeffries who was one of the stars. And that's how we got back together again. We started going together and went together through half of 1946 and 1947, and then we both went our separate ways. We got back together again through very unusual circumstances in 1975.

"I was working for a music publisher, who was the publisher of a song called 'The Tennessee Waltz.' He was actually a country and western publisher. At the time I was dating a jazz clarinet player and I just didn't want any of my friends to know that I was working for a country and western music publisher, because I hated country and western music. I had met a fellow through a girlfriend, who worked down the hall. She too worked for another music publisher; there were a number of publishers in the building, it was on Sunset and Gower.

"One night, after my husband had passed away, and I was working for Rod McKuen, this was in the '70s, I got a call. This fellow identified himself as the owner of a radio station in Hawaii. He identified himself as the fellow who had gone with my friend in 1950, and I thought, 'what in the heck is calling me for?' This was 20 years later. He was succinct: 'I'm here at the Roosevelt Hotel in Hollywood, with a friend of yours, and he would like to speak with you.' And I said, 'Oh, okay.' And so Buddy got on the phone; I didn't know it was Buddy. And he said, 'Hi, Charlotte, how are you?' And I said, 'Uh, I'm fine.' And he said, 'Well, how are things going these days?' And he still hasn't identified himself, and I thought, I don't know if this is someone I really want to know or not, so I was being very circumspect. So soon he said, 'Well, how's your mother?' And I said, 'She's fine,' and I'm thinking, well, this is someone who must've passed mustard at least. And then he said, 'You still don't know who this is, do you?' And I said, 'No. But don't tell me, just give me a clue.' He said, 'Well, how's your son?' And I said, 'Oh, okay.' But I still couldn't guess it! I said, 'Give me another clue. Oh, are your initials CA?' I thought it might have been my old boss at Sunset and Gower, the music publisher. He said no. I said, 'Don't tell me, give me one more clue.' He said, 'You did some Christmas shopping for my sister and my mother.' And I thought, oh no, I never did—and then I drew in a breath and said, 'Buddy Baker?' So he was with this same fellow 20 years ago that he had met through mutual friends of ours in New Orleans. How many chances are there of that happening?

"He had asked this fellow if he knew anything about me, and this fellow said, 'No, but I still talk to a friend of hers. If you'd like me to, I'll call and see if she has Charlotte's number.' I hadn't talked to this girl in 7 or 8 years, but she still had my number, and I hadn't changed it and had not moved. And that's how we got back together again. That was the end of 1975 and we were married the end of 1976.

"My first husband was Bob Davis. He was a singer during the war with Jan Garber who used to sound like Guy Lombardo. He had a swing band. I had gone out on a date with Bullets Durgom who was kind of a road manager/gopher for Tommy Dorsey. We were going to the Aragon Ballroom in Santa Monica to hear Count Basie, and we walked by a ballroom that was within walking distance. It was on a pier down at the beach, it was called Casino Gardens, and Bullets said, 'I want to stop in here for a minute.' I saw Jan Garber and I said, 'Are you kidding?' It was like Lawrence

Welk. He said, 'No, he's got a pretty good band, and I just signed a singer that's with him,' and that's how I met my first husband. It was a series of coincidences. I met Frank Sinatra through Bullets and Bullets later became a manager for some very big names like Barbara Walters and Jackie Gleason.

Buddy conducts a film score.

"Buddy loves to drive. If there is one outstanding thing about Buddy, it's that he loves to drive. He's a very good driver. On a Saturday he would pick me up and we would drive to Riverside which was probably an hour's drive, or we would drive up to the mountains. There was a place called Padua Hills up by Mt. Baldie that had a lovely restaurant out on a plateau. And we would go see musical people, like if Herb Jeffries was around because Buddy did so much work for Herb. We still see Herb here in the Valley. He's 90 now and still sings as great as ever. Wonderful songs like 'Satin Doll' and swinging kinds of music."

Every day Buddy drove himself to work, to Disney or USC, matching the break neck speed or leisurely pace of whatever other Californians were out that day.

Treasure of Matecumbe (1976) is one of the least known of the Disney films of that era, possibly since it's more of a Huck Finn tale with no element of fantasy. Based on the novel by Robert Lewis Taylor, it followed the adventures of two friends, one black, one white, in quest of a buried treasure in order to save their old Kentucky home. Pursued by carpetbagger villains, the boys make it down the Mississippi and through the Florida Keys—it was a lively adventure in the style of *In Search of the Castaways*, but failed to catch on as a true Disney classic, even with plenty of Buddy Baker music heaped upon it. *The New York Times* called it a "literate movie blessed with good actors who seem to be having a good time. [It] finds time to plant a few ideas about the value of education, sanctity of the environment, the repugnance of bigots and the consequences of disrespect for the beliefs of others." The film was double-billed with the semi-classic Disney cartoon, *The Three Caballeros*.

As for his favorite project that Buddy had worked on, be it film or park attraction, Buddy felt more pride "if the thing worked. The best part of the job is finishing a project and seeing that visuals and audio fit hand in glove."

CHAPTER 9
EPCOT

In 1964, Walt Disney had unveiled his experimental prototype community of tomorrow—EPCOT—on television. Walt said it would be a "community of tomorrow that will never be completed, but will always be introducing and testing and demonstrating new materials and systems."

In the late 1970s, Buddy worked in the dull yellow building, marked "Orchestra," on Dopey Drive at Disney's Burbank studios. On loan to the studio from WED, Buddy had been spending the previous two years of his life scoring, overseeing, timing and gathering together other writers, arrangers and musicians for the new theme park, which was split into two main arenas: World Showcase (a variety of countries, all with restaurants and shops; most with attractions), and Future World (huge buildings housing attractions which taught about the world through technology). Buddy was the driving force in everything originally heard there.

Buddy Baker leads the orchestra.

When Buddy was made musical director for the development of EPCOT Center in Walt Disney World in Orlando, Florida, again using his algebraic formulas, he supervised the various composers working on the theme park. And he personally took the helm on seven attractions: *American Adventure, Impressions de France, Kitchen Kabaret, Living with the Land, Wonders of*

China, and *World of Motion*. Though it's now turning more into an offshoot of Disneyworld with its faster rides (*World of Motion* was ditched years later in favor of a car-crashing attraction called *Test Track*) and pop incarnations (*The Living Seas* later splashed into a *Finding Nemo* ride), much of EPCOT's original purpose remains unchanged. One of the most regrettable changes in the Buddy Baker canon comes from the demolishing of *Kitchen Kaberet*, a fun 1940s-type Audio-Animatronics show showcasing The Land's point of good nutrition, to make way for the literally ill-fitting *Soarin'*, an entertaining simulation ride over America via a large Imax-type traveling film as wind rushes through your hair and new age orchestral music (composed by Jerry Goldsmith) plays.

KK could've been called EPCOT's *Country Bear Jamboree*. Sponsored by Kraft, the little robot show tucked into the left-hand corner of The Land taught good health with the help of singing food groups. Proteins Ham & Eggz told corny jokes in the best vaudeville tradition; there was a heated piece of bread rising from the toaster blaring out his "Boogie Woogie Bakery Boy" ("the bread with the sound!") backed by the best supermarket-style Andrews Sisters; there was the laconically Latin "Veggie Veggie Fruit Fruit" from a South-of-the-border salad bowl; it was a hoot.

"My favorite attraction of all that I've done," Buddy said, "and I only did part of the cues in it, is *Impressions of France*. That show has been running since 1982 and it's still the most popular show down there. I added musical scenes to it and used French classical music, like the beach scene at Cannes with bathing beauties and

At the University of Vienna for a seminar, 1995.

all that. I knew that if I had used some famous French composer for that, it would've been a laugh, people would've laughed at it." *Impressions de France* from EPCOT's France was a rich score showcasing famous classical pieces from such French composers as Debussy ("Syrinx"), Offenbach ("Gaiete Parisienne" and "Afternoon of a Faun"), Saint-Saen ("Carnival of the Animals" and "Organ Symphony") and Satie ("Trois Gymnopedies"), weaved together with original Baker music. Its digital score is captivating when heard in its huge room with the five enormous screens (each measuring 21' x 27.5', in a 200 degree circle), stretching out almost but not quite like a Circlevision (filmed with five cameras rather than Circlevision's usual nine). The score was recorded by the 100-piece London Philharmonic, and the result is breathtaking, and it is sure to be the last attraction ever to be replaced in Walt Disney World. The score finally ended up on official Disney park CDs after Buddy's death. He had always wanted a proper release of it.

Buddy's first in line during a break from an EPCOT recording session.

Disney theme park composer Richard Bellis, who worked on music for the Mexico and China attractions of EPCOT (among many others) recalled, "I first met Buddy about two years prior to EPCOT opening at Disneyworld, Florida. Buddy was getting ready to retire and had brought in George Wilkins to prepare to take over his position when he left. George and I had been partners and were close friends.

"One day I got a call from George. 'Hey Bellis, are you busy?' 'Not really,' I replied. 'Good,' said George, 'We've got 90 hours of original music to write and record over the next two years for something called EPCOT.'

"It was while working on that project that I met Buddy. One of the assignments that came directly from Buddy was definitely one of the most enjoyable experiences of my career. In those days, there were people in the music business who were 'arrangers,' not orchestrators but arrangers. Folks who would take an existing song and turn it upside down and inside out and make it sound like a totally new musical entity.

"Buddy called about 6 or 7 of us to do arrangements of several songs written by the Sherman brothers for the Imagination Pavilion. When I asked what he wanted in the way of style or instrumentation or length, Buddy responded, 'This is the Imagination Pavilion. I want all of you to just use your imagination.' That was it. Those were the marching orders.

"The day of recording was incredible. A half-dozen arrangers in the studio all with arrangements that no one had heard before. It was like a jam session for writers with a 70-piece orchestra."

Part of Buddy's challenge was not giving the entire project

the same sound, so he limited his compositional output to just four attractions, working with five arrangers. Most of his work involved conducting and arranging the many traditional songs or new pop tunes that made EPCOT so entirely different from its big brother Disneyworld. Buddy's new arrangement of "Home on the Range" was used, for instance, as entrance music to The Land building so that clues wouldn't be given as to what to expect inside the pavilion.

For the *American Adventure* Buddy recorded music with the Philadelphia Orchestra "since America started in Philadelphia." He recorded other music in London with the National and Royal Philharmonics. At one point he called himself a European at heart, as he loved to travel around Europe for work and pleasure both.

Richard Bellis recalled, "Buddy wrote some great music. Lots of people have written great music. What Buddy left with most of the people he touched was Buddy, the person. Fresh, honest and intimate. You always knew that you were getting the real story from Buddy and not some PC version. "I think Buddy's favorite curse word was 'bullshit.' We were sitting at lunch in the USC restaurant discussing a piece of music written by a young man we both knew. Neither of us was particularly fond of this work and I, trying to legitimize the work, voiced the opinion that the piece was 'a little Bob Marley and a little Phillip Glass' to which Buddy instantly added 'and a lot of bullshit.' "The, now legendary, story I'm sure you've heard is about Buddy, shortly after retiring as an employee of Disney. He was asked to come in and take a meeting about writing some music for one of the theme parks. He was now considered an independent contractor and as such was expected to give the production team a budget. When asked, 'What is this going to cost us, Buddy?' His reply was classic. 'I tell ya what. I'm gonna write the music for free............and I'm gonna charge you fifty thousand dollars to put up with the bullshit.'"

CHAPTER 10
Not Retired

Buddy really enjoyed his last "official" years at Disney, praising the company for giving him such a breadth of material with which to work. Otherwise, he wasn't overly enamored of the current musical trends of the early 1980s. He saw music being written for quantity, not quality's sake. And that for the most part was being written for the young—in a young person's business. Indie bands weren't the moving force they were in the decade that followed, but that was the direction things were going in. Though Buddy's main love was always jazz, he always maintained an affection for "good music," whatever the genre, even rock 'n' roll. "Chicago was good," he said, "but for every Chicago, there are small groups making a lot of loud sounds. There's more jazz going on down in Palm Springs than we can ever find in Los Angeles. It's a nice swingin' town down there. There are restaurants that feature jazz music and we sort of cater to that. I like good jazz."

He admitted to being of the old school: liking to see a properly dressed group on stage, looking like a uniform band. Yet it was this conservatism and knowledge of the history of modern music which caused him to reign as head music man at Disney for so many years.

Buddy, the last staff composer at any major motion picture studio, retired in 1983. "I retired when I did because I could get all my severance pay. Disney didn't fire composers, but it happened at other studios so they couldn't get their severance pay. Since retiring I've been doing work for WDI—Walt Disney Imagineering. I'm not really interested in working with the new people at Disney and the picture end of it. All they're making is—money."

The University of Southern California launched a program in film and television scoring in 1984. Buddy was asked to teach a class in animation scoring the following year, and distinguished himself so well that only three years later he took over as head of the program. So much for retirement.

The program took off and, under Buddy's direction, it became the most eminent department in the country for film and television scoring. Many students are turned away each year, so great is the demand to this day. "The program has grown so big now," said

Doing what Buddy does best.

Buddy, "I'm not even teaching anymore. I'm just running the program. I have 14 instructors working for me down there, and they're the best pros in the business."

Charles Bontrager brought Buddy to Pleasant View Jr. High School on May 3, 1988 as part of a talk to eighth graders on careers in music. While Bontrager geared his talk towards conducting, Buddy took up the subject of timing in music and how precise the marriage of audio and visual had to be. He explained that he would make suggestions at Disney as to what he wanted, but was fully encouraging to let the musicians show their creativity. A question and answer session then followed.

Charlotte, Buddy and Noreene at the 1988 graduation.

Not Retired

> **On May 14th, one of these Disney employees will return to his hometown to conduct the Springfield Symphony.**
>
> HAPPY
> BASHFUL
> SNEEZY
> DOC
> DOPEY
> GRUMPY
> SLEEPY
> BUDDY*
>
> Join us for an evening of Disney magic as United Missouri Bank of Springfield proudly sponsors "Disney Favorites with Buddy Baker," the final concert of the 1988 Symphony season.
> The concert will be enjoyable for the whole family, as Springfield native Buddy Baker returns to play some of the world's best loved music.
> There will only be one performance, May 14, 1988 at 8:00 p.m. in the Evangel Chapel Auditorium. So get your tickets at the Symphony box office today.
>
> *During his 28 years as Music Director for the Walt Disney Studio, Buddy Baker wrote scores for 40 Disney feature films, 125 TV shows and the Disney-on-Parade Arena Show.
>
>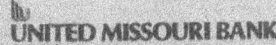
> **UNITED MISSOURI BANK**
>
> 1150 East Battlefield   887-5855   2900 North Glenstone

He told students: "I had learned to write for various instruments over the years. You have to learn all you can and be prepared to use it if you are called on. You might not get a second chance."

On May 14 Buddy conducted the Springfield Symphony in the Evangel College Chapel auditorium. The first half of the program was conducted by Charles Bontrager and featured music from *Fantasia*. Then Buddy led an evening of Disney music, including his own compositions and selections from *Mary Poppins*, *Snow White* and Buddy's *The Fox and the Hound*. During the latter, scenes were projected on three large screens as the music played. Since much of the original Fox orchestrations had not been

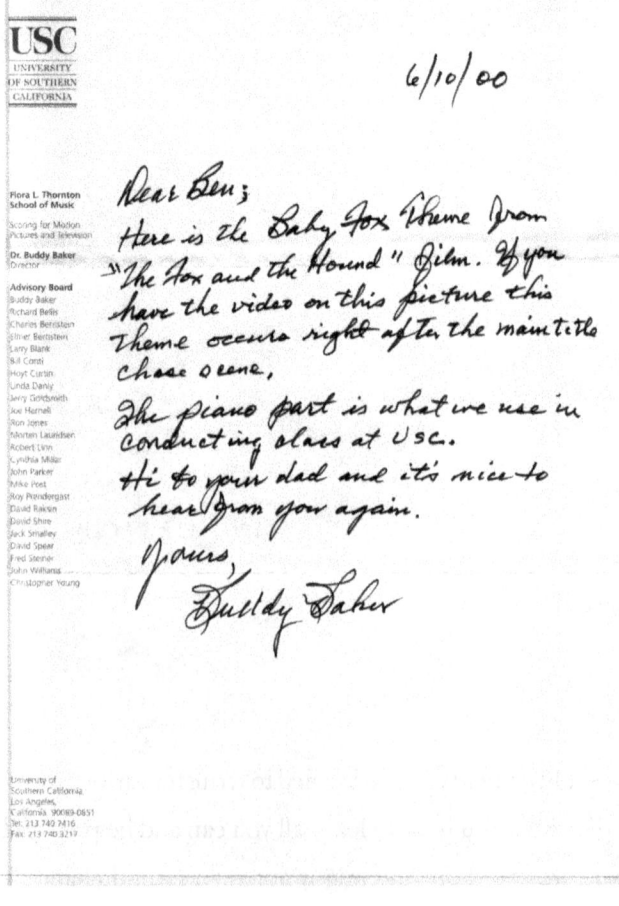

preserved since the soundtrack had first been played for the film, Buddy had to reconstruct much of it for the evening's entertainment. The entire concert began and ended with "When You Wish Upon A Star." After which, Buddy presented Bontrager with a large Mickey Mouse stuffed animal, and Springfield's mayor Tom Carlson declared May 14th to be Buddy Baker Day.

The Symphony had a sell-out crowd that night, with the local paper proclaiming it a triumph. "The idea, the music, the occasion all were delightful and framed a warm and genuine homecoming." A number of Buddy's classmates from Springfield High School were on hand to cheer and wish him well. The paper's review sweetly concluded that "it was a pop concert that really popped."

"If I want to do a concert of Disney music," Buddy explained, "I have to get permission to use my own music, you know. But they've been pretty cooperative on that."

Later that same year Buddy received an honorary doctorate from Southwest Baptist University, along with the Reverend Richard Wakefield, pastor of the First Baptist Church of Camdenton, and Alice Walton, daughter of Wal-mart billionaire Sam, who rather overshadowed the press coverage. "I feel grateful that I've been paid to write music," Buddy said at the podium, "sometimes not much, but sometimes good. It was something I would've done for free. But I never told a producer that." As he smiled and stepped back to take his seat, SBU Chancellor James Sells stopped him. A dozen SBU Chorale members burst upon the stage, removing their top coats and donned mouse ears to sing *The Mickey Mouse Club* theme song. Buddy joined in, as the audience clapped along.

1988 had been a record year for returning alumni and Buddy was happy to revisit the old campus again, talking with other graduates in the Chancellor's Honors Chapel. Naturally they made a fuss about SBU's most famous graduate (Walton's daughter notwithstanding) and Buddy found himself questioned by the school's newsletter for the winter 1988 issue in which he spoke extensively about his Disney career. He also received a Trustee medallion.

He told of his love for walking 1.5 or 3 miles a day to keep in shape, and his love of preserving the old movie music that was often neglected and sometimes thrown away due to poor storage space or conditions.

Heading the program at USC had become one of the most important things in Buddy's later life, if not the most important. His advice to film composing students was: decide on the tempo of the scene first. The most important aspect is to get a dramatic sense of the picture–that is the key to "getting into the picture."

Buddy's last film credit was for *The Puppettoon Movie* (1987), a collection of animated shorts from the master of film effects, George Pal, director of *The Time Machine* and other lavish sci-fi greats. There wasn't much original music needed from Buddy who was hired to score the ends of the film that sandwiched the original shorts. Director/producer Arnold Leibovit created an animated introduction and ending to which Buddy conducted his music with the Graunke Symphony Orchestra.

Music cue from The Puppettoon Movie, 1987.

The music was recorded at Union Studio in Munich, West Germany. Buddy was listed first under Special Thanks in the end credits. A record/CD/cassette of the film's soundtrack was released through Talking Rings Record Company. On the DVD release of the film there is a picture of Buddy with the director in the stills section.

The music, and thrilling opening scene, began much like *E.T.* with its creeping into the forest amidst the lush strings and subtle tension. A single deer eats in a clearing, when Arnie the Dinosaur (voiced by Paul Frees) enters with a loud roar, but turns out to have motivational problems. He just doesn't want to eat the deer, much to director Gumby's chagrin.

The Puppetton Movie, *1987*.

More extravagant music was used during Frees'/Arnie's narration over the brief overview of Pal's career and the main credits, which incorporated the famous "Tuby the Tuba" song (the theme of the film). Buddy's beautiful music carried the film to be something truly memorable.

The Puppetton Movie, *1987*.

In 1998 Buddy was made a Disney Legend by his beloved company for "those individuals whose body of work has made a significant impact on the Disney Legacy." Also in that year's line-up were James Algar (animation director on *Fantasia*, etc., writer of *Disneyland's Great Moments with Mr. Lincoln*, etc.), Kathryn Beaumont (voice of Alice in *Alice in Wonderland* and Wendy in *Peter Pan*), Virigina Davis (early *Alice* cartoons), Don Escen (company treasurer), Wilfred Jackson (animation director on *Dumbo, Song of the South*, etc.), Glynis Johns (Mrs. Banks in *Mary Poppins*), Kay Kamen (marketing director and instigator of the Mickey Mouse watch), Paul Kenworthy (photographer of the popular documentaries, *True-Life Adventures*), Larry Lansburgh (director of the Oscar-winning *The Horse with the Flying Tail*, and others), Hayley Mills (star of *Pollyanna*), Al & Elma Milotte (the married cinematography team behind *True-Life Adventures*), Norman "Stormy" Palmer (editor of the Oscar-winning *Water Birds* and others), Lloyd Richardson (editor of the Oscar-winning *Vanishing Prairie* and others), Kurt Russell (star of the Dexter Riley trilogy and *The Barefoot Executive*), Ben Sharpsteen (producer of twelve of the thirteen *True-Life Adventures*), Vladimir "Bill" Tytla (animator of *Dumbo* and others), and Dick Van Dyke (*Mary Poppins* star).

The Disney Legends honors began in 1988 when Fred MacMurray was the sole name to receive one that year.

"I go to Disneyland usually two or three times a year at the most," Buddy said. "I never go down there for a vacation. Usually it's for an anniversary. X and I signed 1000 posters and 1500 CDs recently of *The Haunted Mansion* score. George Bruns had passed on, so when they redid the *Pirates* ride, I was invited to participate in it, so my name is on the plaque in front of it, for all the additional things I did. Of course George's name is on it as well.

"I can take it or leave it. I'm more interested in how the music works rather than what the ride does. I wrote music for *Space Mountain* and all the thrill stuff at Walt Disney World, and to me the music's kind of lost in there, because people are too excited with the thrill of the ride. The music is part of it, really just a sound effect."

In 1999 Buddy received the prestigious ASCAP Foundation Lifetime Achievement Award, "for his outstanding accomplishments as a composer, arranger, conductor, and mentor in the field of film and television music." Founded in 1975, the ASCAP Foundation "is a not-for-profit organization which promotes and supports charitable and educational programs in the field of music."

One of Buddy's last professional photos.

Even with all these awards, it's difficult to find Buddy's music on CD or as downloads, with the significant exceptions of his theme park songs. "It seems a shame that the Disney Music Company people just had an interest in songs with little or no interest in the dramatic scores," Buddy stated. "Walt always loved the scores because he understood what music did for the picture. I guess the music company had more interest in the songs because the money came in faster. I have no answers to enlighten you about the Disney Music Companies. They have always been a mystery. To have the great talents of composer Paul Smith and the other four of us in the Disney Music family is a mind-boggling question as to why they ignored some of the greatest talent in film music. Oh well, what can you expect? All I know is that I have lost a lot of money from royalties because of their lack of interest."

Regardless, Buddy remained a Disney fan to the very end. "We have seen *The Lion King* on Broadway, actually it's on 42nd Street, and *Fantasia 2000* (I-Max) here in California. I thought *Lion King* was excellent with a lot of imagination. I prefer the original *Fantasia* over *Fantasia* 2000 because I think the original version had much better taste and nothing had to be explained and introduced as it was in 2000."

Late in his life, one of the things Buddy most enjoyed was a long drive to New York City to lead a five-day Buddy Baker Film Scoring Workshop on New York University's Manhattan campus. The program was collaboratively sponsored by ASCAP's Film and Television Music Department, NYU's Department of Music and Performing Arts Professions in the Steinhardt School of Education, and the ASCAP Foundation's Paul F. Cunningham

Fund. The Disney Legend instructed film scoring students on the mechanics of timing and click tracks (audio cues used to synchronize sound recordings to film), but the highlight of the workshop was the opportunity to compose, orchestrate, record and screen a film cue just as Hollywood composers do.

Buddy and Ron Sadoff, 2001.

In the October 2001 issue of ASCAP's *Playback* magazine, a short article with photos from the workshop was run, telling of the previous summer's events. Lectures were held on film music analysis and orchestration, and several workshop seminars were given. "The Business Aspects of Film Scoring" gave a roundtable view on the realities of the business, featuring Stephen Endelman (composer of *Flirting with Disaster, The Englishman Who Went*

Up a Hill But Came Down a Mountain, and others); and Carter Burwell (composer of *Fargo, Being John Malkovich*, etc.) led "The Art of Film Scoring."

Ron Sadoff, NYU's Direct of Film Scoring, was always pleased to have Buddy return. Buddy stated that this new session would be "a prepared agenda devoted to the technique and discipline needed in preparing music cues for motion pictures and television."

Space was limited for the 2001 session. For a workshop fee of $600, "participants will learn the mechanics of timings and click tracks, and the art of composing music for pictures. Over five days, participants will have the opportunity to compose, orchestrate, conduct and record a cue with a live ensemble. On June 6th ASCAP presents The Business Aspects of Film Scoring, featuring a high profile film composer and business executive discussing the business behind the art." And on June 8th "ASCAP presents

The Art of Film Scoring, featuring a high profile film composer discussing the scores from several of his works." All were held in NYU's Frederick Loewe Theatre. If students wished their music audited only (no cues recorded), the fee was $250. Fees went up the following year, with two sets of five sessions offered to meet up with the demand. It was to be Buddy's last session, and his last drive to NYU.

Buddy Baker died shortly after returning, on July 26, 2002. He was 84 years old.

In a series of emails to this author before and after his last trip, Buddy wrote:

5/19/02 3:07:03 PM, Ben Ohmart writes:

<< So how do you like being up North again, now that we're having a cold snap?

It is definitely not California. I have lost my taste for New York City because it's not the vibrant, swinging and fun place that it used to be.

<< Buddy, if you've lost the taste for NY, perhaps you shouldn't make the trip anymore. There are SO many places you and Charlotte could travel to these days. Or do you prefer to go places for a reason?

I love being in New York for these workshops. I'd

love it any place where I'm involved with something musical to do. It's just that New York lacks the class that it used to have. It's a town of raunchy looking people with musical taste to match what they wear.

By the way, was Charlotte having an operation soon? I'd like to call her again, but not if she's recovering from something.

Wrong! I'm the one that may have an operation when I get back to LA to correct a 'leaky' heart valve. Charlotte is OK but she suffers from a condition called Essential Tremor. The same condition that Katherine Hepburn suffers. It's embarrassing for her because of a slight hand tremor. She is searching for some solid relief for it. It is not life threatening.

BB

Buddy from NYC:

The session went OK today. Some real talented students participated and yes, I will think about coming back next year. They are already talking about "next year." This is the 4th year, I think?

Not Retired

I'm grateful to get back on the road again as a little of NYC goes a long way with me. I've driven in New York many times. New York has congestion, Los Angeles has 'traffic.'

BB

His last email to me:

Ben:

We have had a great two week workshop on film music. We finished our second recording date this afternoon and I'll be on my way to California on Saturday. I'll stop off in Springfield, MO. to visit with my sister for an extra day.

Charlotte didn't make the trip since the business she had to attend to came too early for her schedule.

I'll be glad to get back to sunny Calif. and out of this insane madhouse.

Everything in New York City has some sort of little irritating hassle attached. I've seen this place go from a great high class city to a raunchy tourist mecca. I don't want to seem to be an old fogie crank but I'll be happy to get back where the quality of life is better.

Please keep in touch.

BB

After Buddy's death, Charlotte gave his entire music manuscript collection (sketches, lead sheets, conductor scores, etc.) to NYU's Fales Library where it is now housed in its Special Collections. As Buddy told me, "I don't have a lot of 'letters' that I've kept but I do have nearly all my sketches and some scores filed away here in Rancho Mirage. There are about 50 to 58 feature film sketches, over 125 hourly TV shows, and I'd say 40 or 50 theme park attractions, plus some concert scores and sketches."

In 2002, the New York workshop permanently changed its name to the NYU/ASCAP Foundation Film Scoring Workshop in Memory of Buddy Baker.

Rest in peace, Buddy.

Buddy Baker
1918-2002

The Disney company's tribute to Buddy.

Not Retired

A Service of Celebration
for the Life of

Buddy Baker

January 4, 1918
Springfield, Missouri
July 26, 2002
Sherman Oaks, California

Wednesday, August 21, 2002
First Christian Church
of North Hollywood

Time is too slow
for those who wait
Too swift
for those who fear
Too long
for those who grieve
Too short
for those who rejoice
But for those who love
Time is eternity.

Henry van Dyck

TRIBUTES

Al Kasha
(Oscar-winning songwriter and co-songwriter of *Pete's Dragon*)

I worked with Buddy a lot. I have phenomenal respect for him, and I learned two things from him. The words tell you what the instrumentation should be. For example, if you would, say, beat out the drum, he would beat out Da da da Da. He emulated what the words said as much as the music. So when he analyzed the songs that we worked on, he would always analyze the words first, and the music second. So it really penetrated in the public's mind what the words said.

And the other thing he talked a lot about was procity. That means mood of words to music. Like Bacharach would go "the mo-ment I wake up" and he goes up the scale. So Buddy was very aware of movement and mood.

But the other thing I learned too, doing a lot of animation with him, is that things you wouldn't generally do in other pictures you can do here. He would use a lot of 32nd notes and 16th notes. In cartoons, you can do that. For regular features, you would almost never do that.

And with an orchestra, he would use both extremes, from maybe 3 or 4 tubas to strings, harmonizing with instruments you wouldn't ordinarily expect would go together. He was always aware of the humor as well as the drama. Good scoring, he would always say, is that you see the action and then the reaction would be you don't shoot someone before they get shot.

I learned a lot from him and am blessed for it.

Charlotte Baker
(Mrs. Buddy Baker)

He's a very modest man. So when he says, "I was a pretty darned good trumpet player," you know he was.

Buddy is a workaholic. It's a good thing we eat, otherwise I wouldn't see him at all. You have to roll with the punches when you're married to a composer, because they go off in their own little world and do their own thing.

When we got married, I stopped working because he was going back to Florida four times a year, and it would be very hard to walk in and tell people you were going to take off for a couple of weeks every three months. And he would go to Europe on his vacation one of those four times. I missed working. I'm more or less a housewife these days. We have a great dog named Mr. Lucky, which is kind of named after the Henry Mancini song, but also because Mr. Lucky got hit by a truck and I happened to be driving by at the time and saw it and saved his life.

No matter how much of a workaholic Buddy is, he's a wonderful husband. He always remembers birthdays and anniversaries and Valentine's Days and all of those days.

Working for Disney was sort of a dichotomy. On one side, it was wonderful to know you had a steady job, and had a pension, and in some ways, for a musician, to have taken a 9 to 5 job was unusual, because most musicians played and partied all night and slept all day. But Buddy is one of the few who looked toward tomorrow and down the road. So many of the studios, when their composers got close to retiring age, they were fired. So after all those years of work, no pension. But you could always count on Disney. And there were a lot of other perks, like travel. But on the other side of the fence, the producers at that time thought that Disney composers could only write mouse music. Which was so ridiculous. I don't think there's been a Disney composer that has left or retired from Disney that has done a feature picture for another motion picture studio.

Buddy is the oldest working composer in Hollywood. There's David Raksin but he doesn't write for anything anymore. Sadly, Buddy's name is not known outside his peers. Or they mistake him for the race driver Buddy Baker. He said if he weren't a musician, he always wanted to be a jet pilot. And I think he would've been a great one.

Joe Harnell
(Composer of episodes of *The Bionic Woman*, *V*,
***The Incredible Hulk*, etc.)**

Buddy hired me to play piano on a scoring session he did. He was a very distinctive personality, with a humble demeanor. He was like a surrogate father to me, despite the fact that I'm almost as old as Buddy. Over the years he grew to be a mentor and an inspiration in terms of keeping life simple. He would acknowledge that the world wasn't a very nice place, in many cases, but he kept his humor and became so important through the years. His wry smile reminded me of Bob Burns. He was similar to Will Rogers in his demeanor—easy. He was never forthcoming about his emotional or spiritual values. He listened carefully and when he spoke, it was with a minimum of words.

He told me about some business deal he had with Disney to write some music for a project. He asked for a particularly exorbitant amount of money. In a friendly way, with his little grin, he told the executive in charge, "The reason I'm charging you all that money has nothing to do with the music. The money is to put up with your bullshit." And he would say it with a smile, never vengefully or with any major show of emotional resistance. That characterized his behavior in the business world.

When he got involved with USC we had already been teaching at the Grove School of Music. He asked if I would join him. That was around 1990. He loved working with these young people at USC, the enthusiasm they had and he had. He passionately loved the idea of giving away knowledge—if you can't give it away, you can't keep it. With a quiet pride he reported to me that the classes were getting bigger and more successful. Every time we talked there was always a reference to what a good thing it is we're doing. In addition to that, he never thought he ran the show, which is something that most of us are afflicted with, those of us in the arts. Buddy never had an ego. And I never saw Buddy angry. He had a great sense of humor. He was a role model for me, because over the years I had quieted down somewhat. Buddy carried his emotions more gracefully than anyone I've known. He had this enormous energy for being around the young people, especially the ones who were gifted and committed to the notion that the whole business of what we do is a collaborative effort. You don't get to write your concertos on the street.

Buddy never had conflicts about the real world or political aspects on life. I'm a dyed-in-the-wool revolutionary liberal and Buddy was very conservative. He radiated good feelings and he was an inspiration in the fact that he could keep it simple. That was his greatest virtue, as far as I'm concerned.

He also had a love of adventure. The last trip he took, he drove by himself to New York, spent that time there, and came back by himself. He had the best time. He loved to do that. He loved the quiet adventure of seeing the country. He was well-traveled, but wasn't a talker.

Cici Baker
(Buddy's daughter)

He loved his crossword puzzles. He did the *New York Times Sunday* every week. I'm good, but he was better. He was great. I sent him one of the electronic versions, which he liked, but not as much. It was better than nothing. He liked his gadgets, so I sent him an electronic dictionary, too.

He was a solid, calm person as a father. If I got freaked out about anything, he would say, "Everything has a way of working out." I had pneumonia when I was seven. He was in New Orleans working and he came back. He was there. He was always there.

Buddy at home.

Noreene, Charlotte, Buddy and Cici.

My mom always used to laugh because he'd be working in the basement with his headphones on and—I think I inherited this from him—he'd have the TV on and all this stuff going on around him, but he would be writing, so focused that he could do it. To this day I can have the TV and stereo on and if I'm focused, it doesn't matter what's going on around me. He wore the headphones because when you're writing music you're hitting the same notes over and over and you don't want to irritate the whole household. He also had a movieolo at home so he would run the same footage over and over, writing a few seconds of film at a time. Very redundant. He'd do that so he could be home. My mom had a restaurant, a rather hardcore business, and she had to be there. So he was always home.

He was a real people person, and he never changed. He never went Hollywood. He loved the kids and teaching. The students were in such awe because here they were in George Lucas' facilities, recording, and Dad was just sitting there in his turtleneck, drinking coffee. They would all get a segment of film to score. Dad got people from, like, the San Francisco Philharmonic to record it live for them at Lucas, then they played it back with the film segment. If you're going to learn how to write music, you couldn't ask for a better class. After which, we got together to eat Italian food. That was mandatory. We both like garlic and red wine a lot. We'd have veal piccata. We'd walk around. He was a fanatic for pens, which still goes in the gadget file. We'd go down to Michael's art store and look at pens. Mostly he'd buy refills. He was careful with his money. He didn't spend it frivolously at all.

He loved to drive up the coast. He loved fast cars. One night he came home with a Jaguar XKE, a two-seater hotrod. Mom came out, "What are you doing with that!" This was before they drove Cadillacs; he got into the Cadillac phase shortly thereafter. Mom was driving a Buick or whatever. He had that bright red, convertible Jag for a while (early '70s), then it started giving him trouble. Whenever a car started giving him trouble, goodbye! Then he got, even worse, a little MG MGB, a bright red, great car. We loved it and drove everywhere in that thing. He wore a beret and gloves, he was hysterical. When the MG started to give him trouble, he started buying Cadillacs and American cars and I don't think he ever went back. He had every credit card—all Platinum—known to man, but I can't imagine that he would have any balance on any credit card. He liked paying cash.

I think the reason he liked to drive so much was because he liked his own time to himself. Pre-cell phones, it was the one place where he could get away and be totally alone. That's my personal opinion. I say that because that's what I like about driving. We talked about it. That used to be a great thing about flying. For a few hours, you were on your own. He was really comfortable in his own skin. He liked listening to the news while he drove. In the house, it was always the news. When I was a kid in the car, it was always KFWB which is all news, all the time, in Los Angeles.

We used to have a ranch up in central California in the '70s, which we had for quite a few years. We'd drive up there in a Vega, the equivalent of a Honda now, just a good gas mileage car, which was a big thing for him. He loved watching the gas mileage. We'd drive up there every weekend. It was a four-hour drive. They bought the ranch together in the early '70s together. They raised alfalfa, that was the big crop, and they raised pigs, which we used for my mom's restaurant. The contention was that if Mom hadn't had decided to go a different way, we would've raised most of the meat and sold it. We sold most of the alfalfa.

It was about 200 acres in the Paso Palos area, on the Estuary River. I had horses. It was fun. He even had a motorcycle there which he crashed on the first day. Cut his eye, sold the motorcycle the next day. He loved the ranch, but he wasn't a hunter or fisherman or any of that stuff. They sold it because of the divorce. Some of the people who worked at Mom's restaurant worked it and my half-brother, from my mother's previous marriage, worked up there, plus some local hired hands. It took four or five people, because in those days the irrigation wasn't automatic, you had to move the pipe yourself. Most of the grounds grew alfalfa. There was a little grazing area for the cattle. The pigs, which they named after the lead waitresses at the restaurant, were in a nice concrete pig pen.

When he was married to Mom, it was just our house and the ranch. Later, he had the Florida house and the New York apartment which was really nice on the upper East side. Charlotte doesn't like to fly at all. Every time Dad went to New York after the '70s, he just didn't have the same vigor for it, I think because so many of his friends had moved away. He lost his romance for it. The cabaret and jazz scene wasn't the same. He was not a snow person. I live in Lake Tahoe and he would only think about a visit if there wasn't a remote possibility of snow.

Noreene Doss
(Buddy's sister)

He had his medicine stolen on one of his last trips to New York City, but it didn't seem to faze him any. He loves the driving so much and it's relaxing, stopping when he wants to. It's fun for him. He'd usually visit me in Springfield during the drive.

He loves garlic. He's very careful about what he eats. For breakfast I'd fix him Egg Beaters, which is a healthier egg mix. We'd put Worcestershire sauce, liquid smoke and bacon bits in it. It's good, try it sometime! He's handy in the kitchen. He doesn't eat a great deal at one time. He watches his portions more than anything else.

Buddy and Noreene.

We used to have a next door neighbor who came over. Back then there were a lot of people who liked country and western music though we weren't too fond of it. Bud had hooked up this thing to the radio which would block out whatever was playing on the radio when he switched on a microphone that was attached also. When this neighbor came over, country music was playing and the neighbor commented that she hated it. Bud heard that and went back into the bedroom and he pushed the little button. "Now Mrs. Sullens," said the radio, "if you don't like country music, all you have to do is turn off your radio." And she was just horrified! He had a great sense of humor. And he liked knickknacks and trinkets. He loved gadgets, he was a gadget person. When he got things at Christmas that had to be put together, he was good at that. He had tinker toys when he was a kid and he'd build this and that. He had to be using his hands and his mind all the time.

Noreene and Buddy and Mr. Lucky.

CREDITS

(All for Walt Disney Studios, unless noted)

Film

1953   *Wicked Woman* (United Artists)

1956   *I'm No Fool as a Pedestrian* (Jiminy Cricket short)

1956   *I'm No Fool in Water* (Jiminy Cricket short)

1959	*Donald in Mathmagic Land* (Donald Duck short)
1960	*Toby Tyler, or Ten Weeks with a Circus*
1960	*Swiss Family Robinson*
1960	*The Hound That Thought He Was a Raccoon*
1961	*Aquamania*
1961	*Donald and the Wheel* (Donald Duck short)
1961	*Greyfriars Bobby: The True Story of a Dog*
1961	*The Litterbug* (Donald Duck short)
1963	*Summer Magic*
1964	*The Misadventures of Merlin Jones*
1964	*A Tiger Walks*
1965	*The Monkey's Uncle*
1966	*Winnie the Pooh and the Honey Tree* (short)
1967	*The Gnome-Mobile*
1967	*Family Planning* (short)
1968	*Guns in the Heather*
1968	*Winnie the Pooh and the Blustery Day* (short)
1969	*Rascal*

CREDITS

1970   *King of the Grizzlies*

1971   *$1,000,000 Duck*

1971   *Project Florida*

1972   *Napoleon and Samantha*

1972   *Run, Cougar, Run*

1973   *Charley and the Angel*

1973   *Nashville Coyote*

1974   *The Bears and I*

1974   *Superdad*

1975   *The Apple Dumpling Gang*

1975   *The Best of Walt Disney's True-Life Adventures*

1976   *No Deposit, No Return*

1976   *The Shaggy D.A.*

1976   *Treasure of Matecombe*

1977   *The Many Adventures of Winnie the Pooh*

1978   *Hot Lead and Cold Feet*

1979   *The Apple Dumpling Gang Rides Again*

1981   *The Devil and Max Devlin*

1981 *The Fox and the Hound*

1983 *Mickey's Christmas Carol*

1987 *The Puppetoon Movie*

TV

1954 *Davy Crockett*

1954-1988 *Disneyland/The Disney Sunday Movie/Walt Disney Presents/Walt Disney's Wonderful World of Color/The Wonderful World of Disney*

1955 *The Mickey Mouse Club*

1957 *Disneyland: The Fourth Anniversary Show* (Special)

1957 *Zorro*

1958-1959 *Texas John Slaughter*

1958 *The Nine Lives of Elfego Baca*

1959-1961 *The Swamp Fox*

1960 *Daniel Boone*

1963 *Johnny Shiloh*

1965 *Kilroy*

1969 *My Dog, the Thief*

CREDITS

1970   *Menace on the Mountain*

1972   *The Magic of Walt Disney World*

1974   *Carlo, the Sierra Coyote*

1974   *Return of the Big Cat*

1975   *The Footloose Goose*

1977   *Trail of Danger*

1980   *The Kids Who Knew Too Much*

1981   *A Dream Called Walt Disney World*

1985   *Mago de Oz Cuento de Frank Baum*

Video

1984   *Walt Disney World EPCOT Center: A Souvenir Program*

Attractions

Adventure Thru Inner Space

America the Beautiful (CircleVision)

Disney on Parade

Great Moments with Mr. Lincoln

Impressions de France (EPCOT)

It's a Small World

Kitchen Kaberet (EPCOT)

The Mickey Mouse Theater

Pooh's Honey Hunt (Tokyo Disneyland)

Sinbad's Seven Voyages (Tokyo Disneyland)

Space Mountain

The Walt Disney Story

Records

undated	*Star Dust* (Buddy Baker and His Orchestra). Exclusive Records. 78RPM.
undated	*Stars Fell on Alabama.* Exclusive Records. 78RPM
undated	*Two in Love.* Exclusive Records.
1954	*Louie Bellson.* Norgran MGN1007.
1963	*Walt Disney Presents Folk Heroes.* Disneyland. ST-3921. LP
1967	*The Country Cousin.* Disneyland DQ-1306. LP

1967   *Story of the Gnome Mobile.* Disneyland. ST-3946. LP

1968   *Great Moments with Mr. Lincoln.* Disneyland. BV-3981/STER-3981. LP

1969   *Story and Song of* The Haunted Mansion. Disneyland. ST-3947/STER-3947. LP

1971   *Pearl's Pearls* (with Louie Bellson and His Orchestra). RCA/Victor LSP4529.

1972   *Hall of Presidents.* Disneyland. STER-3806. LP

1973   *The World Is a Circle from* Lost Horizon *(and Others).* Disneyland. DQ-1352/STER-1352. LP

1973   *Nashville Coyote.* Disneyland. JMI-4005. LP

1974   *Trick or Treat-Stories and Songs of Halloween* (Livingston)/*The Story and Song from* The Haunted Mansion (Baker). Disneyland. DQ-1358. LP

1974   *America Sings.* Disneyland. DQ-1366. LP

1975   *An Adaptation of Dickens'* Christmas Carol. Disneyland. ST-3811

1982   *Mickey's Christmas Carol.* Disneyland. ST-3825

Awards

Academy Award Nomination (*Napoleon and Samantha*)

Cannes Film Festival (*Donald in Mathmagic Land*)

Country Music Association (*Nashville Coyote*)

Diamond Circle Award from Pacific Pioneer Broadcasters

Grammy Award Nomination (*Songs from The Electric Company; America Sings*)

National Fantasy Fan Club Disney Legend Award (1995)

National Film Advisory Board (*The Best of True-Life Adventures*)

The President's Award from the Society for the Preservation of Film Music ("for outstanding contribution to film music education at USC")

Southern California Motion Picture Council (*Napoleon and Samantha; The Best of True-Life Adventures; The Bears and I; $1,000,000 Duck*)

Writers Hall of Fame of America nominee (posthumous, along with Eugene O'Neill, T.S. Eliot and John Steinbeck)

www.ingramcontent.com/pod-product-compliance
Lightning Source LLC
Chambersburg PA
CBHW051939160426
43198CB00013B/2221